W9-DFN-900

# A Nagging Sense of Job Insecurity

## The New Reality Facing Japanese Youth

## The LTCB International Library Trust

The LTCB (Long-Term Credit Bank of Japan) International Library Trust was established in July 2000, with the liquidated assets of the LTCB International Library Foundation, which was dissolved in the same year, to carry on the original mission of the Foundation which was stated by the founders of the Foundation as follows:

> The world is moving steadily toward a borderless economy and deepening international interdependence. Amid this globalization of economic activities, the Japanese economy is developing organic ties with the economies of individual nations throughout the world via trade, direct investment, overseas manufacturing activities, and the international movement of capital.
>
> As a result, interest in Japan's politics, economy, and society and in the concepts and values that lie behind Japan's socioeconomic activities is growing in many countries.
>
> However, the overseas introduction and dissemination of translations of works originally written in Japanese lag behind the growth of interest in Japan. Such works are not well known outside Japan. One main reason for this is that the high costs involved in translating and publishing materials written in Japanese hinder the undertaking of such activities on a commercial basis. It is extremely important to overcome this barrier to deepen and broaden mutual understanding.
>
> The LTCB International Library Foundation has been founded to address this pressing need. Its primary activity is to disseminate information on Japan in foreign countries through the translation of selected Japanese works on Japan's politics, economy, society, and culture into English and other languages and the publication and distribution of these translations. To commemorate the completion of the Long-Term Credit Bank of Japan, Ltd.'s new headquarters and its fortieth anniversary, LTCB has provided the LTCB International Library Foundation with an endowment.

In pursuing these objectives by way of publishing and distributing the English translations of books written by Japanese authors in the broad fields of Japanese politics, economy, society, and culture, the LTCB International Library Trust hopes to be able to contribute to enhancing international understanding and to the intellectual enrichment of the human community at large.

---

*While the assets management of the LTCB International Library Trust is being handled by the Chuo Mitsui Trust and Banking Company, Ltd., the implementation of the publication project has been entrusted to the International House of Japan, Inc.*

**LTCB International Library Trust/International House of Japan**

# A Nagging Sense of Job Insecurity

## The New Reality Facing Japanese Youth

**Genda Yūji**

*Associate Professor,*
*Institute of Social Science, University of Tokyo*

Translated by **Jean Connell Hoff**

## Transliteration of Foreign Words

The Hepburn system of romanization is used for Japanese terms, including the names of persons and places. Except for familiar place names, long vowels are indicated by macrons. The older Hepburn practice of using *m* instead of *n* before *p, b,* or *m* is followed. An apostrophe is used to distinguish syllable-final *n* from *n* at the beginning of a syllable. The spelling of non-Japanese words that have been incorporated into Japanese reflects the way these words are pronounced by Japanese speakers.

Chinese words are romanized using the pinyin system.

The romanization of Korean words follows the McCune-Reischauer system.

Greek words are transliterated based on the romanization table for the Greek script in the 1997 edition of the *American Library Association–Library of Congress Romanization Tables: Transliteration Schemes for Non-Roman Scripts.*

The local custom of placing the family name first has been followed for the names of Japanese, Chinese, and Korean persons.

This book was originally published in 2001 by Chuokoron-Shinsha, Inc., under the title *Shigoto no Naka no Aimai na Fuan*. English translation rights are reserved by the International House of Japan, Inc., under contract with Genda Yūji and through the courtesy of Chuokoron-Shinsha, Inc.



First English edition published March 2005 by the International House of Japan, Inc.
11-16, Roppongi 5-chōme, Minato-ku, Tokyo 106-0032, Japan
Tel: +81-3-3470-9059 Fax: +81-3-3470-3170
E-mail: saji@i-house.or.jp

Printed in Japan

# *Contents*

# *Preface to the English Edition*

When the bubble economy collapsed in the 1990s, the international assessment of Japan's employment system underwent a huge change. Up to the late 1980s, when I was studying economics in graduate school, virtually all the books and articles dealing with Japanese employment extolled the virtues of Japan's work environment. While the rest of the industrialized world struggled with low growth and high unemployment, Japan alone enjoyed steady economic growth and a spectacularly low unemployment rate. The underlying support for such an economy was thought to be found in the incomparable employment system at Japanese companies.

There was a strong perception at the time that the source of Japan's superb skill development and the high productivity that accompanied it was an employment system that emphasized "lifetime" (i.e., long-term) employment and a remuneration system based on seniority and length of service (seniority-based pay). Countless comparative studies attempted to provide theoretical and empirical accounts of the Japanese-style employment system, the excellence of which was acknowledged worldwide.

In the 1990s, however, that all changed. Confronted by the challenges of globalization and a mountain of bad debts, Japanese companies, unable to make flexible, rapid decisions or take decisive action, continued to stagnate. Long-term employment and a seniority-based pay system came to be regarded as evil practices that these struggling companies were unable to change. In order to catch the next wave and not be left behind, some of them drastically reduced the number of full-time regular employees they hired and made increasing use of part-time and contract workers whose numbers could be flexibly increased or decreased in response to changing circumstances. More and more companies introduced a performance-based pay system that allowed them to raise or lower salaries depending on job performance. Some reform-minded companies loudly bade farewell to lifetime employment and seniority-based pay as the default option.

On the other hand, the attitude remained as strongly entrenched as ever that Japan's highly regarded skill formation system would never be allowed to fade. Conservatives insisted that if the high-value-added route was the Japanese economy's only hope for survival, the Japanese-style employment system, with its emphasis on skill development within the company, would have to be made even stronger than it had been before. Books attacking the introduction of performance-based pay became best-sellers in Japan.

In any event, Japan in the 1990s had lost confidence in itself and had no clear sense of where it was heading. As the economy continued to stagnate, the Japanese media referred to the 1990s as the "lost decade." What had been lost, however, was not simply economic income and wealth. Most Japanese had been deprived of any faith in the future. As Japan's economy toppled from the pedestal it had formerly occupied, its decline in international esteem only intensified the loss of confidence that Japanese felt.

Japanese companies and Japanese society had made catching up with the West their only goal and had achieved economic prosperity by perfecting the Japanese-style employment system. Since the 1990s, however, Japan has graduated from its past experience with success and is searching for ways to cope with the new situation in which it finds itself. Most Japanese, however, are confused as to what goals to set for themselves and how to go about achieving them. The evil consequences of this confusion have, for the most part, fallen on young people.

As the unemployment rate soared in the 1990s, the number of unemployed went up sharply not only among middle-aged and older workers but among young people, as did the number of young people known as "freeters" who do not work as full-time employees but move from one part-time or contract job to another. The increase in these two groups was seen as the result of a change in attitudes toward work among young Japanese. Young adults who continue to live at home with their parents were labeled "parasite singles" and ridiculed as symbols of a weakening sense of self-reliance among Japanese youth, or a growing dependence on their parents.

What lies behind the change in Japanese young people's behavior, however, is not simply a change in the work ethic or a rise in dependence. Rather, these are the by-products of the confusion in the Japanese employment system, which is unable to deal adequately with the new age. Even though, on the surface, a new performance-based system has been introduced, in fact, there has been hardly any change in the way most people actually work. Japanese companies still lack the flexibility to adjust employment, and this defect has manifested itself as a reduction in job opportunities for young people. Conversely, an excessive demand for change has deprived young workers of opportunities for training, which in turn has given rise to young people who move from one part-time or contract job to another. Reduced to the status of social underdogs, Japanese young people have had no alternative but to become economically dependent on their parents.

This book is a record of what actually happened to the employment situation of Japanese young people during the chaos of the 1990s. It documents the upheavals that youth unemployment underwent as Japan plunged from the peak of economic prosperity to the depths of stagnation. I hope this record will serve as some sort of object lesson to those countries that continue to enjoy economic growth today as well as to those that extol the blessings of future prosperity.

Although some of the situations in this book may be unique to Japan in the 1990s, many of the problems it discusses are universal. What can particularly be said to be common to all countries at all times is that, when economic problems occur, it is always the young people who directly bear the brunt of them. At the same time, the only ones who, despite these difficulties, hold out any promise of a brighter tomorrow are the young people who have hope for the future and who constantly and coolly challenge the status quo.

It is a great honor to have my book selected as part of the LTCB International Library Trust translation series. I would like to take this opportunity to express my gratitude to the Selection Committee and the Committee for General Policy of the LTCB International Library Trust. I would also like to thank Jean Connell Hoff for her excellent translation and Saji Yasuo, publication officer at the International House of Japan, who coordinated the project and produced the book.

Genda Yūji
March 2005

# *Prologue*

Two types of uneasiness roil the Japanese workplace: the first is clear cut, the second hard to define. As an example of the first, take the game of bridge: there is always a distinct possibility—apprehension even—that when drawing a card from one's partner's hand it may turn out to be the joker. With an uncertainty of this type its underlying cause can be clearly understood. Another name for it is "risk."

Among the obvious uncertainties about work in Japan today are such threats as mass unemployment arising from efforts to clear up bad debts; a decline in the labour force; globalization and the intensified international competition that comes with it; and technological progress symbolized by the IT (information technology) revolution. Common to each is a clear awareness of what we are up against, even though no sure solution for any of these problems has yet been found. While there are any number of studies and reports that make predictions about, or prescribe policy measures to deal with, these well-defined uncertainties, in this book I would like to direct attention to another source of uneasiness altogether, one that few people are aware of yet is even more serious—a nagging sense of job insecurity.

## Nagging insecurity

To have no clear understanding of why something is happening nor of what will happen next—that is real uncertainty, and that is what I mean by a nagging insecurity. Unlike risk, this sort of job insecurity gives rise to feelings of anxiety for no accountable reason whatsoever.

Emblematic of this vague, amorphous uneasiness is the concern over widening economic disparities. The gap between rich and poor is increasing in Japan, it is said; the middle class is breaking down, and there is a growing polarization between those who are rich and those who are not. The mass media have prepared many special reports on this topic. In May 2000 two of Japan's leading magazines, *Bungei Shunjū* and *Chūō Kōron*, simultaneously published special issues on the growing gap between rich and poor. Recent studies such as *Nihon no Keizai Kakusa* (Japan's Economic Disparities) by the economist Tachibanaki Toshiaki (Tokyo: Iwanami Shinsho, 1998) and *Fubyōdō Shakai Nihon* (Japan, the Inequitable Society) by sociologist Satō Toshiki (Tokyo: Chūkō Shinsho, 2000) have been surprising bestsellers. A sense that the gap is widening pervades Japanese society.

Yet despite this prevailing belief many researchers are quick to point out that such is simply not the case. And certainly when one takes a closer look at the statistical data, it is hard to find proof of growing income inequality. On the other hand, what undoubtedly is spreading through society as a whole is a nagging sense of insecurity about it. And not just about income spreads; many people feel a vague uneasiness about the future of employment and more specifically about their own work opportunities. Although perhaps not precisely what Akutagawa Ryūnosuke (1892–1927) had in mind in his suicide note, "a vague sense of anxiety," with no clear basis in fact, is rampant in Japan. (Akutagawa Ryūnosuke, "A Note to a Certain Old Friend," *Hell Screen; Cogwheels; A Fool's Life*, trans. Beongcheon Yu [Hygiene, CO: Eridanos Press, 1987], 139).

## Young people's problems overlooked

At the end of the twentieth century and the beginning of the twenty-first, the employment problem that Japanese regard as serious is, without question, unemployment among middle-aged and older workers. Employment protection for white collar workers in this age group is invariably treated as an important topic, even as the focus of emergency employment measures. The vast majority of newspaper and magazine articles on employment too are about the problems of older white collar workers. The reason is the rapid spread of job insecurity among middle-aged and older male college graduates working for large companies where lifetime employment has been taken for granted. People who once believed themselves to be members of an elite are elite no longer. The breakdown in this belief has led to a sense of social unease.

On the other hand, as Japanese society ages, not much attention is given to the employment problems that young people face. (For the purposes of this book, "young people" are defined as those in their teens, twenties, and early thirties.) Far less concern is voiced about the present state of youth employment than about the employment of middle-aged or older workers. In fact, however, a number of changes are occurring in youth employment that have never been seen in Japan before. In July 2001 Japan's aggregate unemployment rate reached the five percent level for the first time in recorded history. The unemployment rate for males aged fifteen to twenty-four, on the other hand, has exceeded ten percent every single month since 1999. In September 2001 the aggregate unemployment rate recorded a worst-ever 5.3 percent; the reason: a steep climb in youth unemployment. The unemployment rate for fifteen- to twenty-four-year-old males was 12.4 percent, 1.9 percent higher than the same month a year earlier. By contrast, the unemployment rate for men aged forty-five to fifty-four was 3.6 percent, and the margin of year-over-year increase was a mere 0.1 percent.

In Europe and North America a surge in the number of jobless or unemployed young people is perceived as the principal cause of rising crime and other forms of social unrest. In Japan, however, youth employment is not thought to be all that serious an issue when compared to the employment situation for middle-aged and older workers. Why should that be the case? There are several reasons. The first is the persistent belief that, as Japanese society ages and its birthrate declines, there will be a chronic labour shortage for young people. The surplus of older workers, on the other hand, is expected to become more and more acute. When the first baby boomers who were born between 1947 and 1949 approach mandatory retirement a few years from now, the fear is that the number of unemployed workers in their late fifties and early sixties will reach massive and unprecedented proportions. Compared to this, the unemployment problems of youth are not considered to be serious at all.

The second reason is the contention that youth unemployment is for the most part voluntary (i.e., that young people quit working because they don't like their jobs), and thus altogether different from the involuntary unemployment of older people who want to work but are not able to do so. As a matter of fact, anyone who has studied macroeconomics has been taught that from an efficiency standpoint the sort of unemployment which requires a solution is involuntary unemployment. Youth unemployment, being voluntary, is said not to matter very much from the standpoint of economic efficiency. It is regarded as frictional unemployment, which for the most part arises of its own accord when the labour force shifts from a low productivity sector to one where productivity is high. The frictional unemployment of young people is even regarded as desirable since it increases the efficiency of the economy as a whole.

There is a growing trend at many Japanese companies for pay to be tied more closely to individual performance; wage systems based on seniority are under review. Some people believe that these changing views about the importance of seniority will lead to sweeping improvements in employment conditions for youth. Compared to the harsh employment climate for middle-aged and older workers, it would seem that the future holds no serious problems for young people. But is that really the case?

## Voluntary or involuntary?

Most youth unemployment is said to be voluntary, i.e., chosen of one's own free will. By contrast, most unemployment among middle-aged and older workers is said to be involuntary: they become unemployed whether they want to or not because it suits the convenience of the company they work for.

Classifying unemployment in terms of voluntary and involuntary tends to be regarded as an unequivocal standard of measure, but it actually involves many ambiguities. Allow me to introduce a recent research trend in economics on this very issue. The question, "Why does involuntary unemployment occur?" used to be a central topic in economics, but interest in it has waned significantly. Why? An example found in *Economics*, the textbook written by the 2001 Nobel laureate in economics Joseph E. Stiglitz, clearly sums up the essence of the problem.

Is an unemployed welder in Chicago who has lost his job and fallen on hard times "involuntarily unemployed" because he would like to work at his old welding shop but cannot?

> If the unemployed Chicago welder would move to California and pick grapes, he would have a job . . . . To most economists, and to almost all noneconomists, pinning the label "voluntary" on unemployment simply because an unemployed worker has foregone the option of moving to California to pick grapes is semantic quibbling. The trained welder living in Chicago who is unemployed, while other welders are working, considers himself involuntarily unemployed as a welder. He would be willing to work at the going wage for welders (or perhaps even at somewhat lower wages). But he is justifiably unwilling to relocate to California to become a grape picker. (Joseph E. Stiglitz, *Economics* [New York: W. W. Norton, 1993], p. 713)

Classifying unemployment in terms of voluntary and involuntary is actually extremely difficult. Most methods for measuring the seriousness of unemployment focus on a person's reason for leaving a job—is it at the worker's own initiative or that of the company? This concept is similar to voluntary and involuntary unemployment and involves many of the same ambiguities. If someone is forced to resign because of changes in his/her job description (e.g., deprived of meaningful work or relegated to a desk by the window away from the action), it may not technically be at the company's initiative since the worker was not directly dismissed or the victim of a personnel cut, but can the decision to quit really be said to have been made at the worker's initiative? Since the 1990s the impossibility of analyzing unemployment issues objectively in terms of a worker's free will or initiative has increasingly become the mainstream view in economics.

In that case, the problem is, "Why are young people quitting their jobs?" and we must think back and discover reasons to account for this.

Some people point to changes in young people's attitudes or in their family relationships as the underlying causes behind job turnover among youth. Their values and work ethic have changed, it is said; compared to past generations they have a diminished sense of commitment to work and are less likely to believe it is important. In addition, as the birthrate falls, there has been an upsurge in the number of grown children living with their parents; critics contend that it has become easier for young people to live at their parents' expense, or put bluntly, to sponge off them. As a result they have less need to work for a living and so are more likely to decide to change jobs or join the ranks of the unemployed.

Certainly, the impact of changes in young people's attitudes or in their family environment cannot be ignored. Still, are these really sufficient to make a young person take the plunge and quit his/her job? Another, altogether different reason drives young people to change jobs or become unemployed: they are steadily losing the chance to find meaningful work, work that can provide a feeling of pride and accomplishment. Simply put, most young people do not have satisfying jobs; that is what makes them decide to quit the company they work for.

In addition to changes in the nature of the jobs that are available to them, the exponential increase in the amount of work they are expected to do is another factor behind job turnover among youth. Most companies have been engaging in employment adjustment under the guise of "restructuring." As a matter of fact, however, in almost all cases cutbacks are made primarily by curtailing new hiring, a reflection of just how difficult it is to lay off existing personnel. From the perspective of young employees, however, this means that, as time passes, no one younger than themselves ever enters the company. Consequently the work for those at the bottom of the organization steadily accumulates; it is never ending. Moreover, young workers cannot expect to move up in the company by acquiring more advanced knowledge or skills. A young person who finds him/herself in this situation will one day make the decision to look for another job.

Another reason for the rise in job turnover is that companies provide young workers with fewer opportunities for on-the-job training because they no longer have either the time or money to spare. When workers are deprived of the expectation of developing their talents at their current place of employment, this only serves to reinforce their resolve to quit. For high school graduates in particular, finding work at a large company with a full range of opportunities for on-the-job training is becoming extremely difficult. This promotes voluntary job leaving and accelerates the decline in on-the-job training for youth as a whole.

An increase in the number of young people who voluntarily quit their jobs cannot simply be glossed over by attributing it to a change in attitude or to the ease with which they can sponge off their parents. Still, discussions about employment conditions for young people, especially the surge in job turnovers, it seems to me, tend to be overly optimistic. Workers who find meaningful work while they are young and continue to be challenged by it can take a sense of pride and responsibility in their jobs, and these feelings can invigorate society as a whole. Society, however, is moving in the opposite direction. Many young workers are not acquiring skills or experience and so are losing the will to work. This situation has the potential to generate enormous social costs that can never be recouped.

Nevertheless, the serious plight in which young workers find themselves does not resonate with society. In the past, labour unions have acted as a conduit to convey the concerns of young people and blue collar workers to society at large. But the rate of union organization has dropped so precipitously that this route no longer functions effectively. Instead, the only voice to be given wide currency by the government and the mass media is that which articulates the job insecurities of middle-aged and older white collar workers and other readers of the financial press.

## Transforming uncertainty into risk

Anxiety over income disparities and stress beyond words. Amorphous concerns about voluntary or involuntary unemployment. Restructuring, freeters, parasite singles. Although many Japanese may have a vague sense of the uncertainties surrounding work, most discussions brush these aside and enumerate only the nonessential problems. Books about how to work or the characteristics of a good worker have been cropping up one after another. While their arguments appear to be clear, read carefully they are simply strings of words like "performance-based pay" and "competency" with no precise meaning. Their unclear terminology and expressions, I suspect, probably engender an even greater sense of anxiety.

The present book may not necessarily be what most readers would describe as "easy to understand." Although books on economics which cut through complex social issues have been gaining favor among readers, why has it reached the point that discussions of economics or society must aim only at being easily understood? Of course, I want to be understood, and so abandoning the effort to make my explanations intelligible is out of the question. Still, "easy to understand" does not mean "correct." I suspect it is by no means a minority of us who feel that thinking something is good simply because it is easy to understand is a misguided and dangerous tendency, though one that seems to be growing ever stronger. That is why I feel the need to rely on data to support my ideas. Issues with a close connection to everyday life such as employment and education tend to be a bit scary to deal with because people somehow end up talking about their own personal experiences. For that very reason I will try to grasp the essence of this vague uneasiness from objective facts grounded in solid data.

I have attempted to write this book with salaried workers in their twenties and thirties in mind. It is my intention to describe the working conditions of young people as accurately as possible and to focus in on the root causes of their anxieties. Supporting my argument are a number of empirical economic studies. In "The data speak" section at the end of most chapters, I provide more detailed explanations, as needed, analyzing the data to back up my statements. Readers with no interest in figures or statistics may wish to skip this section. I have tried to write each chapter in such a way that readers can read only those topics that are of interest to them.

It is my hope that by introducing data and actual examples, this book may provide some small assistance in transforming nagging job insecurities into risks that individuals can dispassionately fight.

## *Chapter 1*

# *The Underlying Causes of Job Insecurity*

---

**Question 1**

In Japan, which of the following is largest?
a. the number of unemployed
b. the population of Yokohama
c. the enrollment at four-year colleges

The number of unemployed in Japan rose to an annual average of 3.2 million in the year 2000.

The population of Yokohama, Japan's largest city, is approximately 3.45 million, so the correct answer is b. In September 2001, however, when the unemployment rate was at an all-time high, there were 3.57 unemployed; at that moment the correct answer would have been a. Be that as it may, it would be fair to take the population of Yokohama as a metaphor for the number of unemployed nationwide. (The smallest of the three, by the way, is the number of college students, at around 2.74 million [as of May 2000].) The aggregate number of unemployed in Japan is equivalent to the population of Yokohama and vastly exceeds the number of students attending college, which, it is said, is now open to everyone. When the unemployment rate reaches five percent, it is very difficult to get a real sense of employment conditions in society as a whole from the figures alone; this simple comparison, however, makes it possible to imagine just how many people are unemployed in Japan today.

## The job insecurities of middle-aged and older white collar workers

As employment conditions deteriorate, age- and gender-related differences in unemployment status can be studied by consulting the *Labour Force Survey*, which the Statistics Bureau of the Management and Coordination Agency[1] conducts monthly. From these statistics we know that the unemployment rate for workers in their early sixties is far higher in Japan than it is in other countries. They also show that one reason the Japanese unemployment rate has hitherto been so low was a strong "discouraged worker" effect among women who had lost their jobs and had given up looking for work. By the latter half of the 1990s, however, more and more of these women have been looking for jobs, thereby joining the ranks of the unemployed (Ministry of Labour, *White Paper on Labour*, 2000, 36).

These statistics have deepened our understanding of the structure of unemployment as it relates to age and gender and how this is changing; by contrast, however, there has so far been little discussion about unemployment from the perspective of educational attainment. Whereas age- and gender-related unemployment is surveyed monthly, the relation between unemployment and level of education is studied only in the *Report on the Special Survey of the Labour Force*, which is conducted each year in February and August. The reason this survey is not carried out more frequently is that the response rate plummets when pollsters ask people about their educational background. Even today the undue weight given by society to educational achievement and the inferiority complex many Japanese have on this subject remain as deeply rooted as ever. Discussing unemployment in terms of level of education has therefore tended to be avoided because the data needed to analyze it are insufficient.

---

1. As a result of the reorganization of national government offices in 2001, the former Management and Coordination Agency is now the Ministry of International Affairs and Communications.

Today, however, the relationship between unemployment and schooling is slowly but surely becoming the focus of attention. This new-found interest is closely correlated to public awareness of the job insecurities of middle-aged and older white collar workers. The perception that the employment situation for these workers is becoming more acute is a frequent topic of discussion in the mass media, which regard it as emblematic of the nature of job insecurity as a whole; they have also been singled out in emergency employment measures. Defining "white collar" in terms of occupation, however, is not all that easy to do. Wage and benefit programs at most Japanese workplaces, especially those in large companies, have traditionally been constructed in such a way as to remove any distinction between white collar and blue collar. When it comes to thinking about the job insecurities of white collar workers, in most discussions, among other things, there is a strong underlying assumption that working conditions for middle-aged and older college graduates in management positions are rapidly becoming less secure. In that sense, the distinction between white collar and blue collar is more likely to be a matter of educational background rather than occupation.

As in the case of white collar, it is surprisingly difficult to define how old one has to be in order to be described as "middle-aged and older." According to the standard Japanese dictionary *Kōjien* (fifth edition) *chūnen*, translated here as "middle-aged," is "an age midway between young and old; around forty years old"; *kōnen*, translated here as "older," is defined as "in a high age group; elderly." Another dictionary, the *Shin Meikai Kokugo Jiten* (fifth edition), however, defines *chūnen* as "a classification of people based on age; the years between the midfifties and early sixties," and *kōnen* as "an age at which, by any standards, a person can no longer be said to be young." Thus, there are many different definitions of middle and old age, but since most government employment policies designate "forty-five and over" as middle-aged and older, we will focus on college graduates between the ages of forty-five and fifty-four.

To what extent, then, has the number of unemployed college graduates, particularly middle-aged and older college graduates, increased in the past few years? How central a position do they occupy in the unemployment problem? Let us consider these questions using actual statistics.

**Question 2**

Answer yes or no: The number of unemployed college graduates between the ages of forty-five and fifty-four is greater than the total seating capacity of the International Stadium in Yokohama, where the 2002 World Cup soccer final will be held. Is this statement correct?

## The actual state of unemployment by age and schooling

The most recent data on unemployment by age and educational background (as of October 2001) are found in the above-mentioned *Report on the Special Survey of the Labour Force* for August 2000. The figures are given in table 1-1.

Although the focus of public concern has centered on the unemployment of middle-aged and older white collar workers, in fact a mere 50,000 of the wholly unemployed are college graduates between the ages of forty-five and fifty-four. If that number seems incredible, please refer to table 20 on page 225 of the *Report* for August 2000. This figure is only 1.6 percent of the 3.1 million who were unemployed as of August 2000. To put it in perspective, the maximum seating capacity of the

**Table 1-1 Number of Wholly Unemployed Persons by Age and Educational Background** (As of August 2000; 10,000 people)

| | 15–24 | 25–34 | 35–44 | 45–54 | 55–64 | 65 and over | Total for all age cohorts |
|---|---|---|---|---|---|---|---|
| Primary and junior high school | 10 | 12 | 5 | 17 | 22 | 4 | 71 |
| High school | 28 | 42 | 23 | 26 | 27 | 4 | 150 |
| Junior college and vocational school | 11 | 15 | 5 | 2 | 2 | 1 | 35 |
| College or university, including graduate school | 9 | 15 | 7 | 5 | 6 | 2 | 43 |
| Total for all graduates | 58 | 85 | 40 | 50 | 58 | 10 | 301 |

*Source*: Statistics Bureau, Management and Coordination Agency, *Report on the Special Survey of the Labour Force*

*Note*: Does not include the 90,000 unemployed who are still in school. In cases where the totals do not agree, figures have been rounded off to the nearest whole number; the same is true in the other tables.

International Stadium in Yokohama is 72,370. Unemployed college graduates aged forty-five to fifty-four have attracted much attention as epitomizing Japan's worst employment conditions since World War II, but even if all of them were to assemble at Yokohama's International Stadium, it would still not be full. (Thus the correct answer to question 2 is no.)

On the other hand, if all the 380,000 unemployed junior and senior high school graduates under the age of twenty-five were to converge on Yokohama's International Stadium, which prides itself on being the largest in Japan, more than 300,000 could not get in. Roughly half of the unemployed school graduates, not including those who are still in school, are high school graduates. The next highest group are junior high school graduates, at twenty-three percent. College graduates and those with advanced degrees make up only ten or so percent. Today, as usual, three out of four of Japan's unemployed are high school or junior high school graduates.

## Unemployment among high school grads more serious than among college grads

Even though the ratio of college graduates, particularly middle-aged and older college graduates, to aggregate unemployed may be low, if that ratio has been rising sharply in the past few years, the mounting sense of crisis would be understandable. Therefore, let us compare the situation in February 2000 with that of February 1993 just after the collapse of the bubble economy when the number of unemployed was around half of what it was in 2000. The results are shown in figure 1-1.

Certainly, compared to 1993, the number of college graduates between the ages of forty-five and fifty-four classified as "job leavers" (those who have quit their jobs and are currently unemployed) had risen from 20,000 to 40,000. This is a twofold, or 100 percent, increase. The fact is, though, that the number of unemployed increased by nearly a million during this period, and the vast majority of job leavers were in categories other than college graduates in the forty-five to fifty-four age range. Even if we confine ourselves only to college graduates, those between the ages of thirty-five and forty-four experienced a sixfold rise

## Fig. 1-1 Number of Job Leavers by Age and Educational Background

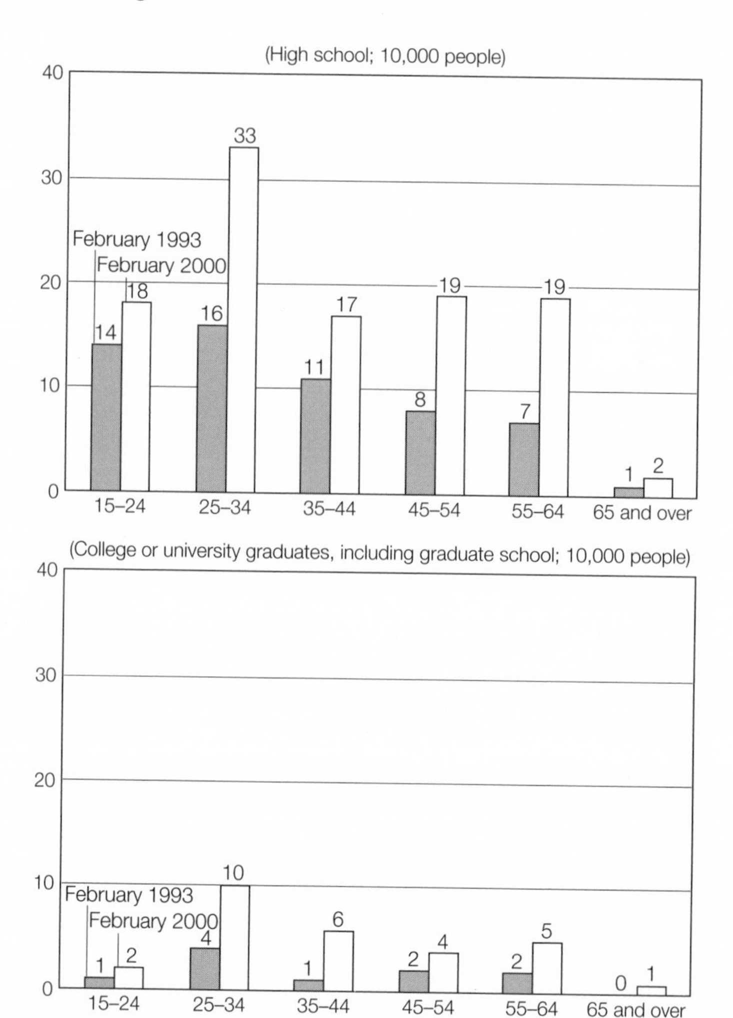


*Source*: Statistics Bureau, Management and Coordination Agency, *Report on the Special Survey of the Labour Force*

*Note*: "Job leavers" refers to those who have quit jobs they had previously held and are currently unemployed. The unemployed may also include workers who formerly were homemakers or students.

in unemployment. Similarly, among forty-five to fifty-four year olds, the rate of increase was far higher for high school and junior high school graduates than it was for college graduates.

If we think about it in these terms, then, despite all the talk about the job insecurities of middle-aged and older white collar workers, it may well be that the deterioration in their employment conditions is being taken far more seriously than the situation really warrants. If that is not the case, then the middle-aged and older white collar workers reflected in the unemployment rate are probably high school and junior high school graduates in management or clerical jobs.

## The future of the labour market

With the sharp rise in the unemployment rate since 1997, employment conditions are said to have become increasingly severe for middle-aged and older college graduates who in the past had been guaranteed stable employment opportunities and secure benefits under a system that was based on long-term employment and salaries tied to seniority. An objective look at the statistics shows, however, that their position in the unemployment statistics has not significantly changed since the early 1990s. Quantitatively, the vast majority of unemployed are still high school and junior high school graduates. And even among this latter group, the distinctive feature of the most recent unemployment picture is that it is not middle-aged and older high school and junior high school graduates who are swelling the ranks of the unemployed but those in their teens to their thirties and those in their early sixties. This means that if we wish to slow down the rise in the unemployment rate, it is critical to provide job opportunities for workers who did not go to college and who are either young or in their early sixties.

Since most unemployment among young people is said to be voluntary, few people regard it as a serious problem compared to the plight of unemployed middle-aged and older college graduates who are finding it difficult to keep up with the cost of living. Young people are criticized for an alleged change in their work ethic, specifically their lack of commitment, which is the motive attributed to them for quitting their jobs; the claim has also been made that Japan's declining birthrate makes it is easier for them to sponge off their parents. Behind the rise in youth unemployment, however, is a factor that has the potential to become a serious social problem in the years ahead. By that I mean the steady decline in opportunities for young people to develop and cultivate their skills through work. It is becoming virtually impossible for recent junior high school and high school graduates to find employment at big companies, which until recently provided opportunities for intensive on-the-job training. Moreover, because downsizing is mostly achieved by cutting back on new hiring, the most routine and repetitive jobs are concentrated on a small group of young employees; companies no longer have the time or the resources to train young workers or develop their skills.

Even though more work may be available for young workers than for middle-aged and older ones, there is a growing polarization between jobs where the working conditions are extremely difficult and those that are too easy and make no demands whatsoever on a worker's skills. This situation is most pronounced for young high school graduates. We have to increase the number of challenging jobs for young people; by that I mean jobs that, though difficult, can give a young person a feeling of pride and joy in his/her work as well as a sense of personal growth once these difficulties are overcome. If this does not happen, Japan, which has attained a high level of productivity through the skills of its human resources, will proceed steadily down the road to stagnation.

**Question 3**

Until last month Ms. A had been seriously looking for a job. She expected to receive an informal job offer, but those hopes were not fulfilled. The shock was so great that she no longer feels like job hunting. Why isn't someone like Ms. A regarded as unemployed for statistical purposes?

## "Unemployed" and "not in the labour force"

"The unemployment rate for last month was . . ." has now become a familiar phrase on the news. Reports that "employment has once again hit an all-time low" bespeak the historically high level of unemployment in Japan.

But is the unemployment rate really the only problem? And precisely what is meant by that term? The unemployment rate is the ratio of unemployed to the total workforce population, in other words, the number of people who, in the last week of each month, have no work whatsoever and are looking for a job, or awaiting the results of a job search, taken as a percentage of the sum total of all employed and unemployed workers. Hence people like Ms. A, who want to work and at one time seriously looked for a job but were unsuccessful and have now stopped looking, are not included among the unemployed. The answer to question 3 is that she has given up searching for a job. People such as this are said to be "not in the labour force." This term is used to signify everyone over the age of fifteen who is neither employed nor unemployed. For most people it conjures up the image of students, homemakers, and elderly retirees, but in fact many people who do not fall into these categories—people who are extremely close to being unemployed—are included in the category of "not in the labour force."

According to the Management and Coordination Agency's *Report on the Special Survey of the Labour Force*, as of February 2001 the number of these people has risen to 41.62 million. Since the entire population over the age of fifteen is 108.35 million, that amounts to 38.4 percent. But among this vast number of people are some who want to work: 9.82 million of them. Just under one in four of those not in the labour force, it is thought, would prefer to work. An even closer look shows that 2.51 million of this latter group have actually looked for work in the past year. If we use our earlier analogy of equating the number of unemployed with the population of Yokohama, then the 2.51 million people who are out of the workforce but have looked for work are equivalent to just a bit fewer than the population of Osaka (as of May 2001 the population of Osaka was approximately 2,605,000).

Many of the people looking for work, whom we tend to imagine are unemployed, are in fact not counted as unemployed but as "out of the labour force." This group, which is equivalent to the population of Osaka, is not included in the reported unemployment rate. Among those aged twenty-five to thirty-four alone, 3.49 million were not in the labour force in February 2001. The majority of these, 1.91 million, want to work. Moreover, 470,000 of them have actually looked for a job in the past year. Since the number of unemployed aged twenty-five to thirty-four in that same period was 870,000, this means that half again as many people in that age group want to work but are not regarded as unemployed.

For a closer look at this situation by age, let us consider the fluctuations in the ratio of those who want to work relative to all those not in the labour force as given in figure 1-2. A glance at this figure shows that the percentage of those who are out of the labour force but who want to work is consistently low in the fifty-five to sixty-four and sixty-five and over age cohorts. These groups bring down the average for all the other age groups. By contrast, from the 1980s on, fifty percent or more of those aged twenty-five to thirty-four and thirty-five to forty-four wanted to work. Moreover, a closer look reveals that by the mid-1990s, the percentage of those out of the labour force who want to work has

**Fig. 1-2 Those Who Wish to Work as a Percentage of All Those out of the Labour Force**

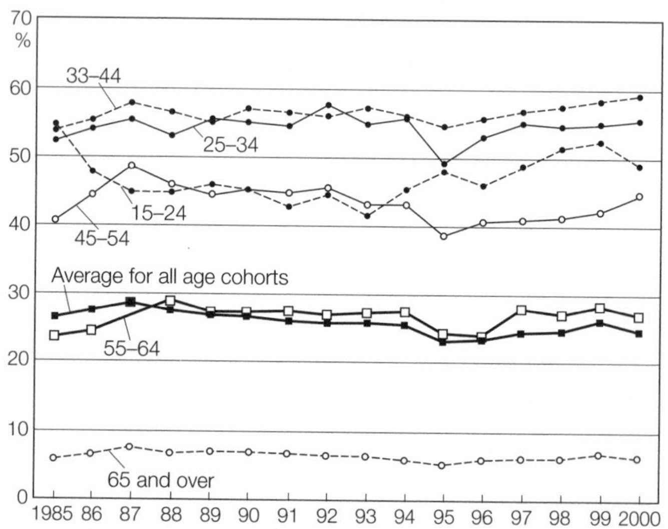


*Source*: Statistics Bureau, Management and Coordination Agency, *Report on the Special Survey of the Labour Force*

been slowly rising among younger age groups, especially among those aged fifteen to twenty-four who are no longer in school. Even among those who are not defined as unemployed, the majority of those who want jobs are in the younger age brackets. That percentage has been steadily rising since the recession of the mid-1990s.

People who want a job but cannot find suitable work for themselves; people who have given up looking for work because job hunting is too tough: situations like these translate into an increase in the number of people—primarily young people—who are not regarded as unemployed but as out of the labour force. Table 1-2 looks at such

**Table 1-2 Number of Those Who Are out of the Labour Force but Who Wish to Work and Have Looked for a Job in the Past Year** (as of August 2000; 10,000 persons)

| Both sexes | 15–24 | 25–34 | 35–44 | 45–54 | 55–64 | 65 and over | Total for all age cohorts |
|---|---|---|---|---|---|---|---|
| Primary and junior high school | 3 | 6 | 4 | 8 | 15 | 9 | 44 |
| High school | 8 | 19 | 19 | 21 | 20 | 6 | 93 |
| Junior college and vocational school | 2 | 13 | 10 | 6 | 2 | 0 | 32 |
| College or university, including graduate school | 1 | 4 | 4 | 2 | 2 | 1 | 14 |
| Total for all graduates | 14 | 41 | 37 | 37 | 39 | 16 | 183 |

| Women only | 15–24 | 25–34 | 35–44 | 45–54 | 55–64 | 65 and over | Total for all age cohorts |
|---|---|---|---|---|---|---|---|
| Primary and junior high school | 3 | 6 | 3 | 7 | 11 | 3 | 32 |
| High school | 6 | 16 | 18 | 20 | 16 | 2 | 79 |
| Junior college and vocational school | 2 | 12 | 10 | 6 | 2 | – | 31 |
| College or university, including graduate school | 1 | 3 | 4 | 1 | 0 | 0 | 10 |
| Total for all graduates | 12 | 37 | 35 | 34 | 28 | 6 | 152 |

*Source*: Statistics Bureau, Management and Coordination Agency, *Report on the Special Survey of the Labour Force*

*Note*: Does not include the 90,000 unemployed who are still in school. In cases where the totals do not agree, figures have been rounded off to the nearest whole number; the same is true in the other tables.

people by age and schooling. As in the case of the table showing the number of unemployed, only a few of them, a mere 20,000, are middle-aged and older college graduates aged forty-five to fifty-four. Of the 1.83 million with school diplomas nearly half—930,000—are high school graduates. By contrast, the number of college graduates is only 140,000. In either case not being able to find a job is undoubtedly a far more serious problem for high school graduates than it is for college graduates.

Furthermore, if we look at this group by gender, the vast majority are women. By the mid-1990s an increasing number of women had moved from unemployed to out of the labour force because like Ms. A they had looked for a job but were unable to find one. In the case of women if we pay attention only to the number of unemployed, we completely fail to understand the problem; the real problem is the 1.52 million women counted as not in the labour force who have looked for but not found work.

Please bear in mind that I am not trying to imply there is anything wrong with Japan's unemployment statistics because some job seekers are counted as out of the labour force. Twenty years ago when the Japanese unemployment rate was conspicuously lower than those of other industrialized countries, some wondered whether there were statistical problems with Japan's unemployment rate because it seemed much too low. And, to be sure, there are minor differences from country to country in the way the unemployed are defined. Today, however, the International Labour Organization (ILO) has drawn up uniform international standards for unemployment statistics, and the Organisation for Economic Co-operation and Development (OECD) calculates and publishes on a regular basis the standardized unemployment rate for each of its member countries. This shows that any concern that the statistics may have been fiddled with because Japan's unemployment rate is so much lower than those of other countries is utterly unfounded. Without going into a detailed explanation here, there are no special problems with Japan's unemployment statistics compared to other countries. (I recommend that those interested read the reports for themselves. See, for example, page 15 of the August 2001 the *Report on the Special Survey of the Labour Force*.)

## Will the unemployment rate go down?

The fact is, however, there is a danger that we may have an excessively optimistic view on the subject of future employment if we look only at the current unemployment rate—because the unemployment rate may fall in the long term.

Will the unemployment rate move steadily upward, or will it unexpectedly go down? To tell the truth, I have no way of knowing. But if we look back at the beginning of the 1990s when everyone was complaining about chronic labour shortages, hardly anyone would have predicted that the unemployment rate would reach five percent. And judging from the bleak economic forecasts, probably no one today believes that unemployment will return to the low levels of the past. But having said that, if we consider the environment surrounding the labour market in the years ahead and look at the unemployment rate from a long-term perspective, it is not entirely out of the question that it will go down. For one reason, it is conceivable that systemic changes, such as those being made to the employment insurance system, will gradually have an effect on the unemployment rate. Revisions are scheduled to be made beginning April 2001 to the length of time during which unemployment benefits will be paid; the benefit period will be extended for those who become unemployed for employer-related reasons such as bankruptcy or closure but conversely will be shortened for those who quit for personal reasons or in the case of mandatory retirement. A special feature of Japanese unemployment is the high unemployment rate for older workers or, to be more precise, for sixty-year-olds immediately after mandatory retirement. The generous unemployment benefits retirees have hitherto received have been criticized as a "second severance payment." When the benefit period is shortened, it is possible that the number of post-retirement unemployed will decline. Shortening the time during which retirees are on the unemployment rolls, thereby accelerating their departure from the labour market, will in effect reduce the unemployment rate for sixty-year-olds.

Changes in the demography of the labour market as a whole may also produce downward pressures on the unemployment rate. A high unemployment rate among older workers may be characteristic of

Japan, but, as in other industrialized countries, the highest rate of all is among young workers. In 1999 the rate for teenaged males climbed to fifteen percent in Japan compared to an OECD average of seventeen percent. (For more details see Mitani Naoki, "Jakunen Rōdō Shijō no Kōzō Henka to Koyō Seisaku" [Employment Policy and Structural Change in the Youth Labour Market], *Nihon Rōdō Kenkyū Zasshi* [Japanese Journal of Labour Studies], May 2001.) As the birthrate goes down and the population ages, it is possible in the long term that the percentage of young people will decline, and the result of this demographic change will be to bring down the aggregate unemployment rate. As a matter of fact, a study shows that the drop in the US unemployment rate from the mid-1980s through the 1990s was for the most part due to a decline in the youth workforce. This study suggests that a rise in the U.S. incarceration rate, which includes large numbers of young males with a high potential of becoming unemployed, has also contributed to a decline in the unemployment rate (L. F. Katz and A. B. Krueger, "The High-Pressure U.S. Labour Market of the 1990s," *Brookings Papers on Economic Activity*, no. 1 [1999]: 1–88).

Although there is no way of predicting what will happen to Japan's crime rate or its prison population, it is entirely possible that a drop in the birthrate will bring about a decline in the percentage of the youth workforce, which in turn will bring about a reduction in Japan's aggregate unemployment rate.

## A country where only one out of every two works

Speaking of employment problems, the only thing anyone pays any attention to is unemployment. But, as we have seen, that is not the only problem. The distinction between unemployed or out of the labour force notwithstanding, the truly important issue is that everyone who wants to work be able to do so.

Some Japanese have expressed concern recently about the increase in the number of "freeters"—those who cannot (or will not) become full-time employees. (For more on "freeters" see chapter 3.) In the long run, however, the important consideration is not whether someone is a full-time employee but that he/she in some form or other has the opportunity to work. What complicates matters when thinking about work opportunities is that the distinction between unemployed and out of the labour force is becoming blurred. For statistical purposes the out of the labour force population is divided into "housework," "in school" or "other." Although the number "in school" has decreased, this has been more than made up for by a continuous rise in the categories for "housework," and "other." As a result, the annual average has risen from 36.57 million in 1990 to 40.57 million in 2000, an increase of exactly four million over the course of the 1990s. Of these the number classified as "other," i.e., those neither engaged in housework nor attending school, had increased by 3.26 million, from 11.4 million in 1990 to 14.66 million in 2000. The vast majority of these people had probably once worked and had looked unsuccessfully for a new job but have now given up.

The determining factor as to whether someone who is not working is considered to be unemployed or out of the labour force is whether he/she is looking for a job. "Looking for a job" does not necessarily entail going to Hello Work (the public employment security office) or buying help-wanted magazines, however. As long as an individual considers him/herself to be looking for work, he/she is unemployed. Conversely, if someone had at one time looked hard for a job but couldn't find one and has now given up, he/she is out of the labour force, not unemployed. As job search methods such as the use of the Internet proliferate, many cases are likely arise in which it is unclear even to the individual him/herself whether he/she is actually looking for a job or not.

When the borderline between unemployment and out of the labour force is blurred, it makes it difficult to grasp how serious the employment situation may be from the unemployment rate alone. For that very reason, we need a simpler, more objective indicator to reveal what the employment situation really is. The ratio of the employed to the population aged fifteen and over is, I believe, a suitable candidate to serve as just such an indicator. Figure 1-3 shows changes in the employed population rate since 1953. The "employed" referred to here include executives, agricultural workers, self-employed, domestic help, those doing piecework at home, those with side jobs, part-time workers, those on secondment, and all others who are working except full-time

**Fig. 1-3 Number of Employed as a Percentage of the Population over the Age of 15**

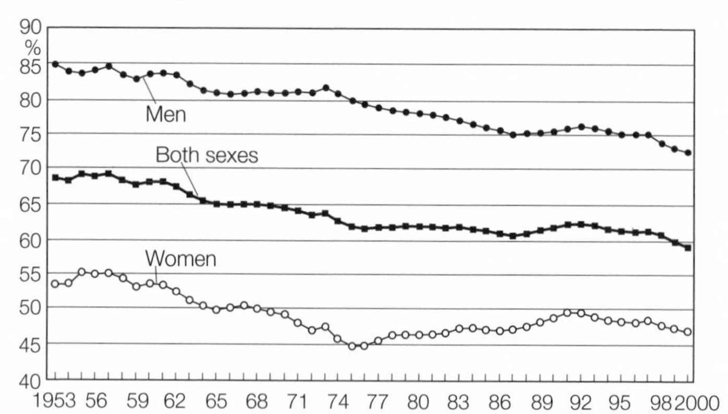


employees. As the result of an aging population, more students going on to higher education, and the shift from manufacturing to service industries, the employed population rate has been steadily declining over the long term.

If the trend continues at its present pace, by a simple estimate Japan will become a country where fewer than one person out of every two aged fifteen and over works. Just for women alone, the rate will dip below forty percent by 2050. Even for men, it is expected to drop to one person out of two in 2099 (for further details see "The data speak" at the end of the chapter). There is something indescribably unnatural and unhealthy about a country where fewer than half the adult population works. Can this situation be changed? What needs to be done to change it? The growing segment of the population aged sixty and older holds the key to what employment will be like in the years ahead. If Japan can create an environment in which more of the elderly who are out of the labour force would like to work, the employed population rate will go up. But older people who have worked hard all their lives may be looking forward to a carefree retirement and may not want to work anymore. Is it really fair to force them to go back to work?

But even more significantly, there are lots of young people who want to work but do not or cannot—not just those who are unemployed but also those who are considered to be out of the labour force. Among them are many women and high school graduates who have a latent desire to work but have not yet been able to fulfill that ambition.

What precisely is preventing young people from finding jobs? I shall consider the reasons for this in the next chapter.

## The data speak

## Why will only one out of two Japanese be working in 2050?

Let us assume that the annual employed population changes over time at a fixed rate. By using past data we can estimate what this pace will be. To be more specific, it can be thought of it as the following equation:

$$\text{employed population rate} = \text{constant} + (\text{rate of change}) \times \text{year}$$

Our focus is on year as the major factor affecting the employed population rate. A variable like year, which produces an effect, is called an "independent" or "explanatory" variable; a variable affected like employed population rate is called a "dependent" variable. To make an estimate it is necessary to know the constant and the rate of change that determine the annual employed population rate.

Though it is only an estimate, that does not mean it is all right to make a blind guess; and so we look for a criterion that is statistically reliable. This is the "least squares criterion." Fluctuations in the real and the estimated employed population rate (total for both sexes) are given in figure 1-4. Though the estimate is reliable, inevitably there will be a

Fig. 1-4 Estimate of the Employed Population Rate (Both sexes)

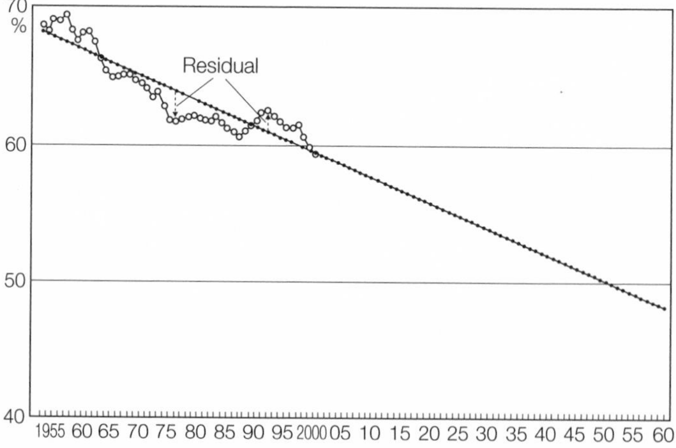

margin of error between the real value and the one predicted. This margin of error is called a "residual"; as the figure shows, it can be plus or minus.

But for an estimate to be valid, the absolute value of the residual, whether plus or minus, will probably be small. When the residual for each year is squared, the values of the constant and the rate of change that minimize the sum of the residual squares are considered the most suitable for the estimate. The method of seeking a valid relationship by this criterion is called "ordinary least squares."

Specific uses of the least squares method are always explained in econometric textbooks. Anyone with even a very basic knowledge of differential calculus can find the constant and the rate of change. Here the constant obtained is 4.2900 and the rate of change is minus 0.001848. From the rate of change the employed population rate is thought to decline each year by approximately 0.2 percent. The rate of change for each sex can also be found using the same method. The results are given in table 1-3.

But even when results obtained are statistically valid, they can vary from slightly to highly valid. Therefore a "coefficient of determination" is calculated to measure the degree to which the equation is valid. The coefficient of determination takes a number between zero and one; the

**Table 1-3 Results of a Regression Analysis of the Employed Population Rate**

| | Employed population rate | | |
|---|---|---|---|
| | Men | Women | Both sexes |
| Year | | | |
| Coefficient | –0.002377 | –0.001409 | –0.001848 |
| (t-value) | (–31.59) | (–6.50) | (–15.75) |
| Constant | | | |
| Coefficient | 5.4892 | 3.2778 | 4.2900 |
| (t-value) | (36.90) | (7.65) | (18.50) |
| Coefficient of determination | 0.9559 | 0.4789 | 0.8436 |

closer to one, the more valid it is. In this case, the coefficient of determination is 0.8436, which is a comparatively high value.

In some cases, however, it is doubtful whether the values obtained for the constant and the rate of change are really statistically reliable. When a straight line is estimated but the deviation of the estimated value from the real value is extremely large, the value obtained is unreliable. As a matter of fact, the year may have no effect on the employed population rate; in short the rate of change may be zero.

To determine whether or not the value of the coefficient is really zero, a method in statistics known as the "t-test" is used. In table 1-3 a t-value is calculated for each coefficient. In cases where the absolute value of the t-value exceeds two, the value of the coefficient will not be zero, and it is regarded as definitely having an effect. In this particular case the t-value is 18.50 for the constant and minus 15.75 for the rate of change, both greatly in excess of two. For that reason the figures 4.29 and minus 0.001848 are thought to be reliable. In the language of statistics, these results are said to be statistically significant.

From this valid equation, which has been shown to be statistically reliable, it is possible to predict the long-term employed population rate for the twenty-first century. For example, the employed population rate for both sexes in the year 2050 would be

$$4.29 + (-0.001848 \times 2050) = 50.16(\%)$$

From this result it is estimated that if the present pace continues, only one out of every two Japanese over the age of fifteen will be working (or able to work) in the mid-twenty-first century.

# *Chapter 2*

# *The "Parasite Single" Explanation*

## Worsening youth employment

The employment environment for young people is deteriorating. Since the late 1990s youth unemployment rates have risen sharply: between 1999 and 2000 the average annual unemployment rate for males under the age of twenty-five exceeded ten percent; the rate for the month of September 2001 was the worst on record at 12.4 percent. The Japanese unemployment rate has overtaken that of the United States and is now considerably higher particularly for workers in their twenties.

Nevertheless, the job insecurities of middle-aged and older workers remain a far greater cause for concern in Japan than those of young people. One reason for this is that the increase in youth unemployment, at least for now, is not linked to a significant rise in the crime rate. Studies show, however, that even in Japan there is a close correlation between labour supply and demand and the incidence of crime. There is an undeniable possibility that Japan may one day become a high crime society depending on what happens to youth employment.

Job insecurity among middle-aged and older workers has been taken far more seriously in Japan than the employment situation for young people. Senior white collar workers in particular are thought to have suffered massive job losses as a result of corporate restructuring. But is it really true that employment has worsened for these workers? As we saw in the preceding chapter, a mere 50,000 of the unemployed were college graduates between the ages of forty-five and fifty-four; this accounts for less than two percent of the total 3.1 million who are unemployed. The vast majority of the rise in unemployment is in fact concentrated on young people and those over sixty; the employment situation for middle-aged and older workers on the whole is not as grave as it is reported to be.

Why isn't youth unemployment taken more seriously? The answer is that most unemployment among young people is thought to be voluntary. As we shall see in greater detail in the next chapter, despite successfully making it through a freeze on hiring in the mid-1990s which was so severe that it was known as the "ice age," seventy percent of the junior high school graduates, fifty percent of the high school graduates, and thirty percent of the college graduates quit their job in three years or less. Not surprisingly, middle-aged and older workers in the throes of their own job insecurities are quick to decry the wasteful frequency with which the younger generation changes jobs.

What is behind the increase in unemployment and job turnovers among young people? Most discussions focus on young people's attitudes and home environment. Their values and work ethic have changed, it is said, and they no longer feel any commitment to work. As the birthrate falls, it also said to have become easier for grown children to live at home and sponge off their parents. When critics bewail the decline in young people's work ethic and cite this as the cause of their rising unemployment and job-turnover rates, the discussion invariably turns to the "parasite single" explanation.

## What is a "parasite single"?

A "parasite" is an organism that lives off another organism; the word also refers to an insect that does so. What then is a "parasite single"? Allow me to introduce an excerpt from *Parasaito Shinguru no Jidai* (The Age of the Parasite Single) (Tokyo: Chikuma Shinsho, 1999) by sociologist Yamada Masahiro. A parasite single is "an unmarried child who lives with his/her parents even after graduation and is dependent on them for his/her basic living conditions." According to calculations

Professor Yamada made based on the national census, the number of men and women aged twenty to thirty-four who are unmarried and still living with their parents has soared to ten million. These "parasite singles" represent a growing trend in Japan. Reluctant to lower their standard of living by getting married or living on their own, they choose instead to maintain their present high living standard by continuing to live with and be dependent on their parents. The increasing number of parasite singles in Japan, he claims, is the basic reason behind the country's fast-rising trend toward later marriages and the decline in the birthrate.

International comparisons show that Japan has the highest percentage of single young adults living with their parents.[1] The main source of financial support for post-adolescent young people takes different forms in the advanced industrialized countries, ranging from the Swedish model of reliance on the government to the American model, which provides no safety net; the Japanese model, Yamada claims, is characterized by the continued reliance of young adults on their parents. The emergence of parasite singles can be attributed both to social and cultural factors unique to Japan as well as to political and economic reasons. The major factor among the former is the strong parent-child relationship. Self-reliance tends to be undervalued by Japanese parents "who will do anything for their children." The political and economic factors Yamada cites include company-related employment practices such as seniority-based pay and lifetime employment that favor middle-aged and older workers. These have had an impact on the growth of parasite singles, as does Japan's social insurance system, which provides generous benefits to the elderly.

The emergence of parasite singles also casts a shadow on Japan's changing youth labour market. Since these young people do not face

---

1. However, the number of young people living with their parents has also been increasing in the United States and Canada between the 1970s and 1990s. See David Card and Thomas Lemieux, "Adapting to Circumstances: The Evolution of Work, School, and Living Arrangements among North American Youth," *Youth Employment and Joblessness in Advanced Countries,* eds. David G. Blanchflower and Richard B. Freeman (University of Chicago Press, 2000).

economic hardship, they have no need to look for a high-paying job and instead take a dilettante-ish attitude toward work. If they find their job uncongenial, they have no hesitation about quitting. The youth unemployment created in this way is "luxury" unemployment since it has no serious economic consequences. For parasite singles a job is nothing more than a discretionary pastime or a way to earn pocket money.

Despite the rise in youth unemployment and the decline in on-the-job training for young employees, neither is considered a serious social problem. The reason for that, Yamada says, is the emergence of the parasite single.

## Misperceptions about youth unemployment

The expression "parasite single" no doubt accurately encapsulates the changing circumstances in which Japan's young people find themselves. In particular it is a highly suggestive metaphor for the situation facing some young women living in urban areas.

From an economic perspective the impact of the parasite single phenomenon on the labour market can be understood as a change in the values and behavior of the young people who are the suppliers of labour services, in other words as a supply-side shock. Also in line with the parasite single argument is the contention that most unemployment and job turnover among young people are voluntary and result from an unwillingness to work. As a matter of fact it is probably true—although there is no clear statistical analysis to support it—that a long-term rise in unemployment rates is more or less affected by changes in workers' attitudes and home environment. But can the rapidly deteriorating state of youth employment since the mid-1990s really be explained in terms of a supply shock? Attitudes and home environment do not change as precipitously as this. Isn't the drop in corporate hiring coupled with a steep decline in the economy, in other words, a demand-side shock to labour services, a more important consideration?

In order to consider structural changes in employment during the 1990s from a perspective other than unemployment trends, let us look at the ratio of regular employees to the total labour force population (figure 2-1). ("Regular employees" are defined as executives or those under

**Fig. 2-1 Ratio of Regular Employees Relative to the Total Workforce Population**

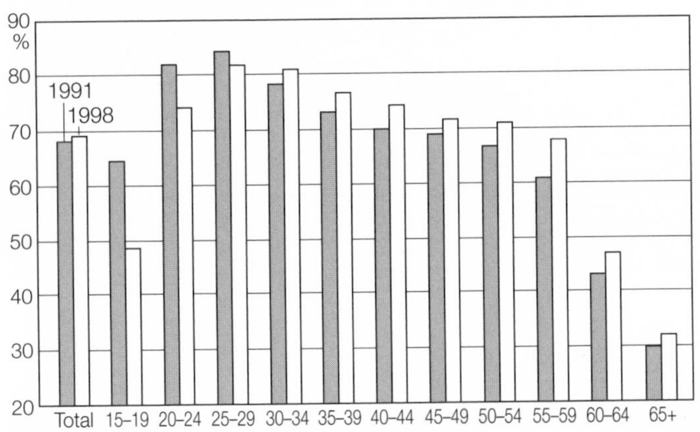


*Source*: Statistics Bureau, Management and Coordination Agency, *Annual Report on the Labour Force Survey*

contract for at least a year or for an unspecified term of employment. Those not defined as regular employees are temporary workers or day labourers.) Although much has been made about the diversification of employment patterns in Japan, the proportion of regular employees actually rose, albeit only slightly, between 1991 and 1998. In terms of age groups, however, the percentage fell for workers under thirty. Fewer than one in two teenagers were regular employees, and the rate for those in their early twenties went down by nearly seven percent. On the other hand, it increased for all age groups over thirty; for those in their late fifties it went up by seven percent, the exact opposite of what happened to those in their early twenties.

It is possible, of course, to construe these changes as signs of an increasing resistance to regular employment among young people. But isn't a decline in employment opportunities resulting from a drop in labour demand the more natural explanation? No matter how hard I try, I cannot come up with any conceivable reason why young people should show a growing preference for jobs with limited prospects (if wages for temporary workers or day labourers were notably higher than they are for regular employees, it would be quite a different matter).

Once a contract ends, most people regardless of age would prefer to avoid if possible the sheer awfulness of looking for a new job.

One indication of changes in labour demand can be seen in the age-related fluctuations in the employment rate at large companies. This rate is a proxy indicator of the willingness of large companies (which generally offer high salaries) to hire new help. It has been declining for each new cohort; the rate for teenaged hirees is now more than ten percent lower for the cohort born in the early 1980s than it had been for the cohort born in the late 1950s. The truth is that it is becoming extremely difficult for a high school graduate to become a full-time employee at a large company. For a long time the percentage of employees in their early twenties was over twenty percent, but it has now fallen far below what it had been for the cohort born in the early 1970s, which includes the second baby boom generation (those born between 1971 and 1973). These figures give an inkling of the worsening employment environment for young people due to the steep drop in labour demand at large companies.

Cutting back on the hiring of young people has often been resorted to in the past during temporary economic slumps. But the current, ever-worsening decline in youth employment opportunities is not a temporary phenomenon due to recession but is becoming a long-term structural problem. Behind this structural change is the steady aging of Japan's workforce and the vested employment rights that middle-aged and older workers continue to hold firmly in their grip.

## The repercussions of an aging workforce

Japanese companies, especially the large ones, are experiencing a rapid aging of their workforce. At large companies with more than 1,000 employees the ratio of those aged forty-five and over to the total number of full-time male employees has increased from thirty-one percent in 1991 to thirty-seven percent in 2000. Back in 1979 after the second oil crisis it was only twenty-two percent. This comparison gives us a good sense of how steeply the percentage of middle-aged and older workers has risen over the medium to long term.

The graying of the workforce is undoubtedly the cause of job insecurity among surplus middle-aged and older workers. One reflection of this growing labour surplus is the fact that the wage structure for middle-aged and older college graduates at large companies is showing signs of change. Their salaries are slowly decreasing relative to those paid to young college graduates and to middle-aged and older high school graduates. Moreover, wage differentials are steadily widening among middle-aged and older college graduates themselves.

The sense that there is a surplus, indeed a saturation, of middle-aged and older workers has not led to a steep reduction in their numbers, however, but rather to drastic cutbacks in the hiring of young people, primarily recent graduates. In other words, to compensate for letting middle-aged and older workers hold onto the jobs they already have, employment opportunities are being taken away from young people. This can be called a "displacement effect" or a "vesting effect." What I mean by "displacement" is a situation in which middle-aged and older workers continue to occupy positions they received in the past, thereby stealing jobs that by right young workers ought to be doing.

As a matter of fact, large companies with a high percentage of full-time employees aged forty-five and over are most likely to cut back sharply on the number of job openings for recent graduates. The very fact that they have a high proportion of older workers reflects three structural factors confronting these companies. The first is that they hired huge numbers of young people during the period of rapid growth; the mass hirees of the early 1970s were entering their late forties and fifties in the late 1990s. These aging workers are a factor behind the ever-increasing personnel costs at companies unable to change their seniority-based wage systems.

Secondly, many companies with graying workforces have been cutting back on the employment of young people since the oil crisis. Because these workplaces have continued to reduce hiring since the 1970s, employees below the age of forty-five make up a smaller component of their workforce, and as a result the proportion of those over forty-five is rising. Reduced hiring is not just the result of the recession in the 1990s; it has been going on for a much longer period of time.

Thirdly, these companies are finding it increasingly difficult to offload middle-aged and older full-time employees onto other companies. If transfers between a parent company and its affiliates *(shukkō)* can be made on a large scale, companies can farm out their surplus older workers, thereby reducing the proportion of workers aged forty-five and older at their firms. Because they can no longer do so, that proportion is rising.

These structural factors have given rise to the displacement effect that has caused most large companies to curtail all youth hiring. Figure 2-2 shows the results of an analysis I made of the factors determining the number of available job openings for those expecting to graduate in March 1997. The study focused on private sector workplaces with more than 500 employees as of June 1996. To be more specific, figure 2-2

**Fig. 2-2 By How Many Percentage Points Does the Estimated Number of Job Openings for Recent Graduates Decline When the Ratio of Workers 45 and Older to Regular Employees Rises by 1 Percent?**

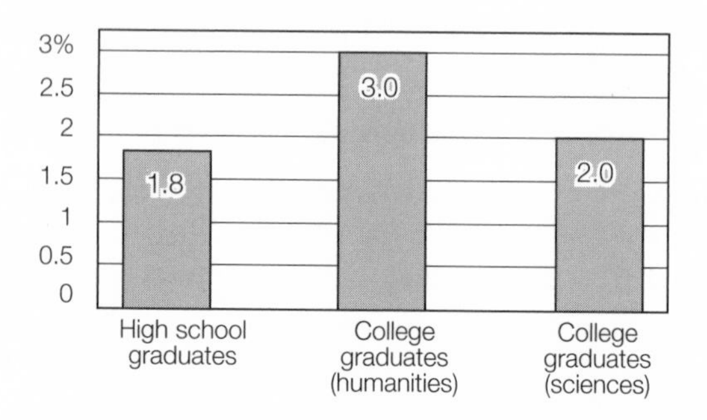


*Source*: Calculations taken from Genda Yūji, "Who Really Lost Jobs in Japan? Youth Employment in an Aging Japanese Society," *Labor Markets and Firm Benefit Policies in Japan and the United States*, eds. Ogura Seiritsu, Tachibanaki Toshiaki, and David Wise (Chicago: University of Chicago Press, 2003). The establishments studied were private workplaces with 500 or more employees. For details about how the estimates were arrived at, see "The data speak" section at the end of the chapter. For workplaces that expected to have an average number of job openings, the analysis sought to find by how many percentage points the number of openings were reduced by a one percent rise in the proportion of workers aged 45 and older.

shows by how many percentage points the number of openings for graduates at each level of schooling is reduced when the proportion of employees over the age of forty-five increases by a single percentage point. For example, a one percent increase reduces the number of vacancies for recent high school graduates by 1.8 percent. The impact manifests itself even more clearly in the case of college graduates. The decline in job openings for college graduates is particularly noticeable for those in the humanities; it is two percent for science majors but more than three percent for humanities majors. For the analytical method and the data used to obtain these figures, see "The data speak" at the end of the chapter.

## Employment practices and the labour market

Some distinctive and notable features of Japanese employment practices and Japan's labour market lie behind the displacement effect. The first of these is the seniority system. Although seniority is gradually losing some of its importance at Japanese firms, it remains as deeply entrenched as ever as a wage determinant especially at large companies. Since the seniority system remains essentially intact, the graying of the workforce is triggering an enormous rise in labour costs. Reducing the number of older employees who are the cause of spiraling personnel costs, however, itself generates considerable expenses for businesses. If they let workers go, they are unable to recover the huge human resource investments they have made as a result of on-the-job training. Consequently, even if business performance is deteriorating, companies that value skill development are most likely to try to avoid layoffs as much as possible.

In addition, companies that try to fire employees face tough legal restrictions. Under case law establishing the doctrine of the abuse of the right of dismissal, if they dismiss workers, particularly in the case of retrenchment, they have to satisfy the following four requirements: (1) they must have excess personnel; (2) they must have made every effort to avoid redundancies; (3) they must have a rational selection process for the workers being dismissed; and (4) they must demonstrate due concern in their separation procedures (for further details see Suwa

Yasuo, *Koyō to Hō* [Employment and the Law] [Tokyo: Hōsō Daigaku Kyōzai, Nihon Hōsō Shuppan Kyōkai, 1999], particularly chapter 9). According to the 1999 edition of *Employment Outlook*, which the OECD publishes annually, Japan is regarded as having some of the strongest employment protection laws in the OECD. Furthermore, mass layoffs may have the effect of lowering a company in society's estimation and give it a reputation for having no compunction about firing its employees. No company can afford to disregard this kind of "reputation effect." As a result of all these considerations keeping middle-aged and older workers on the payroll is an economically rational decision despite the concomitant rise in labour costs.

Under the circumstances, the only means left to achieve optimal employment levels should business performance worsen is to reduce employment by reassigning workers within the company or by transferring them from the parent company to its affiliates and, if neither is possible, to cut back on new hiring. Until the mid-1990s large companies could adjust their employment levels by encouraging the transfer of surplus workers to small and medium-sized companies where labour demand was high. The recession of the late 1990s, however, unlike earlier ones, greatly reduced the demand for labour even at small and medium-sized firms. Thus large companies have had no choice but to trim the number of entry-level openings.

Recruiting fewer young workers does not lead to an immediate reduction in employment levels, however. Economics textbooks tell us that when there is a decline in demand, flexible adjustment to price will ensure a regular supply. Japan's youth employment market, however, is far from this sort of ideal. To be sure, when supply and demand is tight—in a "sellers' market"—some wage adjustments such as a rise in starting salaries may occur, but wages are not adjusted downward in a "buyers' market" when supply and demand is slack (Ishikawa Tsuneo, *Income and Wealth* [Oxford: Oxford University Press, 2001], chapter 6). The result is a classic situation described in Keynesian economics: in response to an excess labour supply, it is not wages but only employment that is cut back.

The situation in which young people find themselves differs from Keynesian economics in one regard; although it is involuntary, society as a whole, and even in some cases the young people themselves, regard it as voluntary. Middle-aged and older people who make up the majority of society are implicitly aware that a closer examination of the decline in youth employment would threaten their own employment status. Thus they dare not say that youth unemployment isn't really the young people's own fault. Young people themselves are not fully aware that opportunities for long-term employment and skill development through on-the-job training are far fewer now than they were for young people in the past (i.e., today's middle-aged and older workers). They avoid thinking about it altogether on the grounds that there is nothing they can do. They give up hope. For young people who find themselves in this situation, the employment environment is indeed deteriorating, and the "parasitism" of the younger generation is by no means the cause.

**The relation between youth employment and parasite singles (1)**

The decline in youth employment is triggered not by changes in the labour supply but by a major decline in labour demand as companies keep their middle-aged and older workers on the payroll. The "parasite single" is not the cause but the consequence of rising unemployment rates and other changes in the employment environment for young people.

The problem is structural: young people are no longer being offered employment opportunities at large companies where wages are generally high, long-term employment is the norm, and individuals can develop their skills through on-the-job training. As the possibility of finding a job with long-term prospects declines, young people feel less commitment to the jobs at which they are currently employed, and this leads to unemployment and job turnover. This situation is fraught with danger and may one day lead to a decline in Japanese productivity.

**The relation between youth employment and parasite singles (2)**

The deteriorating employment opportunities and rising unemployment rate for young people cannot be explained by changes in the labour supply implicit in the "work as pastime" argument. Not all youth unemployment is frivolous unemployment of the "luxury" kind.

## The entrenched vested rights of middle-aged and older workers

The following sentence is found on page 188 of *Parasaito Shinguru no Jidai*:

> Parasite singles have what might be called vested rights. They depend on these vested rights in the form of their wealthy parents and are unwilling to give them up. They cling to them yet all the while dream that something even better must be out there somewhere.

The ability of children to continue to exercise the right to live with their parents and be financially dependent on them for a long time is said to be characteristic of parasite singles; the term is not applied to less well-off parents and children who live together in order to save on the cost of living. The fact that children can exercise this right is predicated on the assumption that their parents are wealthy. In Japan, parents' wealth is assessed on the basis of the assets they own; naturally enough, this amount is affected by the earnings they receive from working. And their vested right to acquire these earnings is protected by a complex network of social and economic systems.

One of the wage determinants for middle-aged and older employees, the seniority system, is changing only gradually. This is clear from the comparison of the age-earnings profiles of employees and the self-employed in figure 2-3 (self-employment and the possibility of starting one's own business will be considered in chapter 8). Earnings in Japan used to be based on seniority not only for hired workers, i.e., employees,

**Fig. 2-3 The Age-Earnings Curve for White Collar Employees and the Self-Employed**

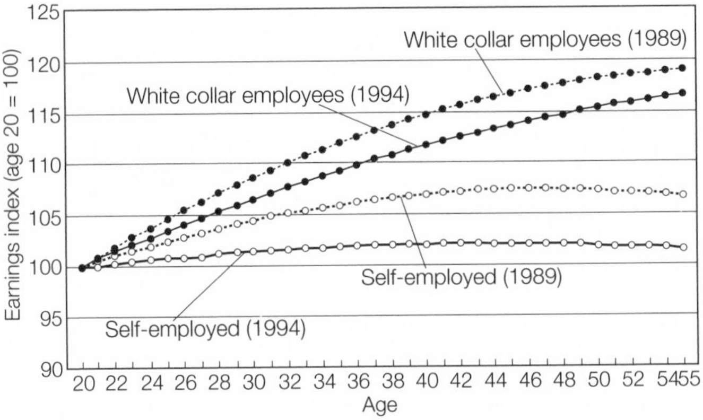

*Source*: Genda Yūji and Kambayashi Ryō, "Declining Self-Employment in Japan," *Journal of the Japanese and International Economies* 16 (March 2002): 73–91

*Note*: In addition to age and type of occupation, asset holdings were used as a control. The possibility of a sample selection bias was taken into consideration, and Hechman's two-step procedure was used to make the estimates.

but even for the self-employed; they reflected the accumulation of experience and would increase with age until around fifty or so.

The self-employed are strongly exposed to changes in the market environment, however, and growth in the seniority component of their income virtually disappeared between 1989 and 1994. This was particularly noticeable among the self-employed in metropolitan areas who experienced the collapse of the bubble economy. By contrast, seniority-based pay for employees is protected by a number of systems within their companies, so its decline has been gradual. Not as much progress has been made in dismantling the seniority wage system as is generally claimed.

As for long-term employment also known as "lifetime employment," the reality is that it has actually been gaining strength among middle-aged and older workers. A glance at the statistics shows that the average number of years of continuous service at the same company is on the rise. In addition, the proportion of "lifetime employees" in their fifties (people who have been employed at the same company since graduation) increased from the 1980s through the early 1990s (Chūma Hiroyuki, "Keizai Kankyō no Henka to Chūkōnensō no

Chōki Kinzokuka" [Changes in the Economic Environment and the Long-term Continuous Service of Middle-Aged and Older Workers], *Koyō Kankō no Henka to Josei Rōdō* [Changes in Employment Practices

**Fig. 2-4 Average Number of Years of Employment at the Same Firm**

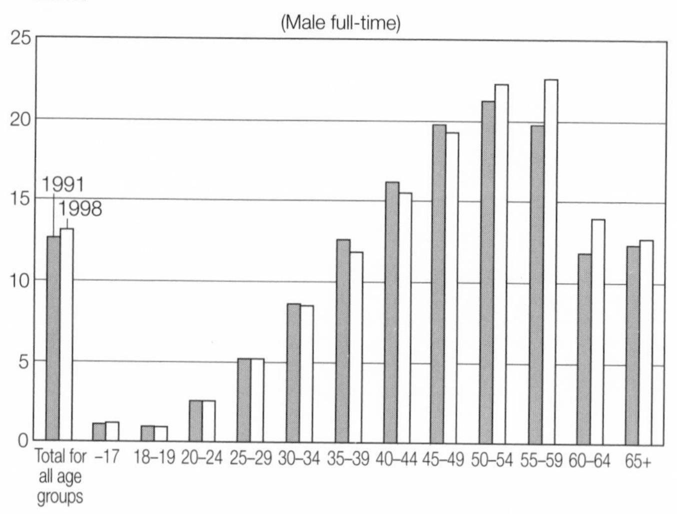


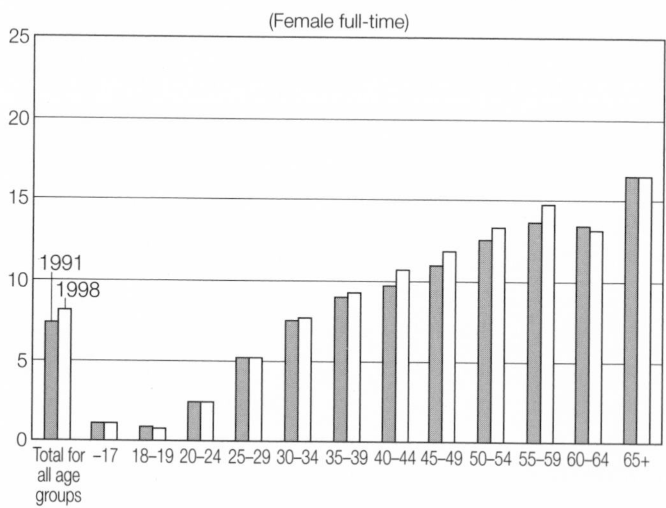


*Source*: Ministry of Health, Labour and Welfare, *Basic Survey on Wage Structure (Wage Census)*

and Female Labour], eds. Chūma Hiroyuki and Suruga Terukazu [Tokyo: University of Tokyo Press, 1997]).

Young people nowadays, it is said, lack a commitment to work and quit as soon as something unpleasant happens. The statistics, however, do not indicate that the number of years that young full-time workers spend at a single firm has been getting any shorter. As figure 2-4 shows, the average job tenure for men and women in their twenties and early thirties has remained virtually unchanged throughout the 1990s. On the other hand, it has been increasing among men over fifty. This trend is the exact opposite of popular opinion, which is firmly convinced that long-term or lifetime employment is on the wane.

The government is planning to extend the mandatory retirement age to sixty-five as part of its employment policies for the elderly. When Japan's baby boom generation—those born between 1947 and 1949—begin retiring in 2007, the call to extend the retirement age or abolish it altogether can be expected to grow even stronger. If that happens, and other systems remain unchanged, the displacement effect will be even further intensified. Reinforcement of the vested rights that protect the jobs of middle-aged and older workers will take even more employment opportunities away from young people. The social security system is also biased against youth since deductions for income and health insurance are now only permitted for people with dependents. And surely the likelihood is extremely low that case law related to the abuse of the right of dismissal will be modified to make it easier to let existing employees go. Thought about in these terms, it is clear that in Japan it is not only the labour unions as in Europe that

**The relation between youth employment and parasite singles (3)**

Contrary to the belief that parasite singles enjoy the vested right to live at their parents' expense, the real parasites are the parents, the generation of middle-aged and older workers on whom society has conferred vested rights and who make their livelihood at the expense of young people.

protect the vested rights of middle-aged and older workers but a whole complex web of social and economic systems.

There is little pressure to dilute these rights; if anything, the direction in which Japanese society is currently heading is to maintain or strengthen them even further.

## No hope for the future

Opinion polls on the future of Japan conducted at the end of the twentieth century invariably elicited pessimistic responses. "Japan will be worse off in the future," or "Japanese living standards will steadily deteriorate" were typical. Despair about the future is deep rooted among young people. Where does this sense of powerlessness come from?

Young people eventually become middle-aged, and then old. In the past they were able to hope that even though they were having a tough time now, if they just had patience, they would be well-off in the future. Revisions to existing systems and practices have been postponed, however, because of the high costs they entail, allowing middle-aged and older workers to maintain the status quo and making it more and more likely that when the tough measures are finally taken they will adversely affect the middle-aged and older workers of the future, i.e., today's young people. How can the young have any hope for the future under these circumstances? If young people show an increasing tendency to live off their parents, this cannot be attributed to emotional problems such as a decline in self-reliance or in the willingness to work. Rather it is the product of a socio-economic structure that attempts to preserve or even reinforce the existing vested rights of middle-aged and older workers.

Efforts to improve the work environment and increase productivity will be of little use unless the vested rights now lavishly bestowed on the older generation are abolished. Ensuring work opportunities for young people who are always being shunted aside on the pretext that they lack a work ethic—that would be true social justice.

## The data speak

### The graying workforce and hiring trends

The late 1990s witnessed a huge decline in employment opportunities for younger age groups. This trend was particularly noticeable at large firms. What kinds of companies experienced a marked drop in employment opportunities? If we accept the displacement effect hypothesis, then those where the graying of the workforce is well under way would seem to be most likely to restrict the hiring of young people in order to protect the employment of middle-aged and older employees. Is it possible to confirm this hypothesis from the statistics?

The *Employment Trend Survey* conducted annually by the Ministry of Health, Labour, and Welfare gathers information on all workplaces with more than 500 employees (more than seventy percent of these are large firms that have 1,000 employees or more). We will use the detailed report published in 1997 to clarify the form that employment adjustment takes at large companies.

As our explanatory variables, we will focus on those that indicate the composition of permanent employees in the workplace, i.e., the ratio of workers aged forty-five and over, the proportion of white collar workers (= the percentage of clerical or management positions), female employees, part-time employees, and transferees. We will also take into consideration such factors as company size, location, and industrial sector.

The dependent variables are the hiring rate and the separation rate—the number of full-time or part-time workers who were hired, let go, or transferred to an affiliated company *(shukkō)* or reassigned within the firm *(haichi-tenkan)*—taken as a percentage of the total number of current employees. As in chapter 1, we will use the least squares method to make a regression analysis of the impact of the explanatory variables on the dependent ones. The results are shown in table 2-1.

The significant variable is the ratio of workers aged forty-five and over. When that ratio rises by a single percentage point, the hiring rate for full-time employees drops by 0.0510 percent. Since the t-value, which measures the reliability of the figures, is minus 5.64 and the absolute value is well above two, the result is statistically significant (on the t-value, see "The data speak" in chapter 1.).

The table's findings confirm that a workplace with a high proportion of older workers is most likely to resort to every possible means to reduce its hiring rate. Such firms have a strong tendency to hold down inflows by reducing full-time hiring and the number of *haichi-tenkan* within the company. *Shukkō* also decrease. On the other hand, the absolute value of the t-value for outflows (i.e., separations or internal transfers) of full-time employees is less than two. There is thus no evidence that the number of people leaving workplaces with a large proportion of older workers is on the upswing.

**Table 2-1 Results of a Regression Analysis on the Determinants of**

| | Hiring rate | | | | |
|---|---|---|---|---|---|
| Explanatory variables | Full-time | Part-time | *Shukkō*[3] | *Haichi-tenkan*[4] | Full-time |
| Ratio of employees 45 and over | –0.0510 (–5.64) | –0.0165 (–4.07) | –0.0049 (–4.17) | –0.0529 (–2.80) | –0.0310 (–1.76) |
| Ratio of management and clerical workers | –0.0337 (–5.33) | –0.0094 (–3.30) | 0.0000 (0.02) | 0.1287 (9.71) | 0.0132 (1.07) |
| Ratio of female employees | 0.0718 (8.66) | –0.0124 (–3.35) | –0.0014 (–1.31) | –0.0329 (–1.89) | 0.0398 (2.46) |
| Ratio of part-time workers | –0.0656 (–5.11) | 0.3281 (56.98) | 0.0013 (0.78) | 0.0081 (0.30) | –0.0519 (–2.08) |
| Ratio of *shukkō* | –0.0103 (–0.29) | –0.0119 (–0.75) | 0.1502 (32.03) | –0.1392 (–1.87) | –0.1070 (–1.54) |
| Sample size | 2,094 | 2,904 | 2,904 | 2,904 | 2,904 |
| F-statistic | 33.09 | 355.74 | 85.17 | 29.29 | 7.15 |
| Adj. $R^2$ | 0.125 | 0.613 | 0.273 | 0.112 | 0.026 |

*Source*: Fifth Employment and Human Resource Development Research Organization (labour market working group) (March 2001) of the Japan Institute of Labour in the old Ministry of Labour.

*Notes:* 1. The data used in this analysis were taken from the establishments studied in the *Employment Trend Survey* for 1996. Those studied were private sector workplaces with more than 500 employees. The method used was the least squares method. The t-values are given in parentheses.

2. In addition to those given above, the explanatory variables include a constant, a metropolitan area dummy (either Tokyo, Osaka, Aichi, Kanagawa, or not), a company size dummy (100–999 or 1,000 or more), as well as dummies for major industrial sectors; the impact of differences in region, company size and industry was not considered. Further details can be found in Genda Yūji, "Who Really Lost Jobs in Japan? Youth Employment in an Aging Japanese Society," *Labor Markets and Firm Benefit Policies*

Although a high proportion of employees aged forty-five and older does not promote layoffs, on the other hand, it does greatly reduce hiring. These results are perfectly consistent with the displacement effect. In addition, workplaces with a high proportion of white collar workers and a low proportion of women are most likely to cut back on new full-time hiring.

The foregoing regression analysis was carried out on the assumption that labour flows at large workplaces would have little impact on employee composition such as the percentage of workers forty-five and over. It is possible, however, that massive inflows or outflows may affect that percentage. Or to put it another way, some readers may think that the relationship is the reverse: that since the proportion of older workers has increased because the hiring of new graduates and other young people has been reduced, the very fact that there are many workers forty-five and older has led to a reduction in hiring.

As a way of getting around this problem, we take the ratio of job openings for new graduates relative to the number of current employees as our dependent variable and analyze it against the same independent variables found in table 2-1. By using this method there is no need to worry about a reverse relationship since the increase in the number of vacancies has no effect on the proportion of forty-five-year-olds and older.

The data are taken from the 1996 *Employment Trend Survey*, and the dependent variable is the

**Labour Hiring and Separation Rates**

| Separation rate | | |
|---|---|---|
| Part-time | *Shukkō*[3] | *Haichi-tenkan*[4] |
| –0.0100 | –0.0033 | –0.0147 |
| (–2.85) | (–3.09) | (–1.88) |
| –0.0102 | –0.0003 | 0.0941 |
| (–4.13) | (–0.49) | (17.07) |
| –0.0082 | –0.0018 | –0.0155 |
| (–2.55) | (–1.90) | (–2.15) |
| 0.2836 | 0.0025 | –0.0142 |
| (56.43) | (1.65) | (–1.27) |
| –0.0051 | 0.1660 | –0.1080 |
| (–0.36) | (39.48) | (–3.48) |
| 2,904 | 2,904 | 2,904 |
| 353.66 | 127.40 | 105.41 |
| 0.612 | 0.361 | 0.318 |

*Japan and the United States*, eds. Ogura Seirits, Tachibanaki Toshiaki, and David Wise (Chicago: University of Chicago Press, 2003).

3. "*Shukkō*" refers to transfers and returns across firms.
4. "*Haichi-tenkan*" refers to transfers within a firm.
5. Both the F-statistic and the adjusted coefficient of determination (Adj. $R^2$) are indicators to measure the ability to explain the estimate equation as a whole.

number of job openings for those expecting to graduate in March 1997. The survey was taken at the end of June 1996. Vacancies were put at zero for workplaces which at that time replied they were not hiring; those that were undecided were eliminated from the sample. The method used to make the estimates was the tobit model. The results are shown in table 2-2. If the proportion of workers over the age of forty-five rises one point, openings for high school graduates are reduced by 0.0300. The t-value is minus 4.71 and is statistically significant. Similarly, the estimated coefficient of the ratio of workers aged forty-five and older is negative and statistically significant at each educational level. Once again it is statistically possible to confirm that workplaces where the graying of the workforce is well advanced have reduced their vacancies for new graduates. The rate of reduction shown in figure 2-2 is sought as an estimated value (0.0300) of the proportion of those forty-five and older to the mean value of the proportion of openings for recent graduates (in the case of high school graduates, 0.0164).

At large workplaces, including most big companies, aging workforces and rising adjustment costs for existing employees are linked to a reduction in the number of job openings for recent graduates. The existence of this sort of displacement effect can be confirmed by empirical analysis.

The above analysis was made possible thanks to the special permission I received to recalculate the government statistics found in *Employment Trend Survey*, as part of the Fifth Employment and Human Resource Development Research Organization (labour market working group) (March 2001) of the Japan Institute of Labour in the old Ministry of Labour.[1] The details are explained in my article "Who Really Lost Jobs in Japan? Youth Employment in an Aging Japanese Society," *Labor Markets and Firm Benefit Policies in Japan and the United States*, eds. Ogura Seiritsu, Tachibanaki Toshiaki, and David Wise (Chicago: University of Chicago Press, 2003).

1. As a result of the reorganization of national government offices in 2001, the former Ministry of Labour is now the Ministry of Health, Labour and Welfare.

**Table 2-2 Determinants of the Estimated Number of Job Openings Relative to the Estimated Number of March 1997 Graduates**

| All recent graduates | High school graduates | Special school graduates | Vocational school and junior college graduates | College graduates and post graduates | Humanities majors | Science majors |
|---|---|---|---|---|---|---|
| Ratio of employees 45 and over | –0.0300<br>(–4.71) | –0.0367<br>(–2.91) | –0.0210<br>(–3.08) | –0.0447<br>(–3.16) | –0.0377<br>(–3.26) | –0.0268<br>(–3.23) |
| Ratio of management and clerical workers | 0.0102<br>(1.89) | 0.0189<br>(2.13) | 0.0245<br>(5.53) | 0.0895<br>(9.73) | 0.0536<br>(7.81) | 0.0495<br>(9.23) |
| Ratio of female employees | –0.0055<br>(–0.79) | 0.0213<br>(1.83) | –0.0032<br>(–0.46) | –0.0145<br>(–0.99) | –0.0268<br>(–2.21) | 0.0038<br>(0.44) |
| Ratio of part-time workers | 0.0005<br>(0.05) | –0.0498<br>(–2.94) | –0.0081<br>(–0.79) | –0.0082<br>(–0.38) | 0.0099<br>(0.60) | –0.0229<br>(–1.69) |
| Ratio of *shukkō* | 0.0065<br>(0.32) | –0.0623<br>(–1.43) | –0.0347<br>(–1.44) | –0.0337<br>(–0.91) | –0.0931<br>(–2.06) | –0.0078<br>(–0.38) |
| Sample size | 1,095 | 403 | 731 | 933 | 783 | 856 |
| LR $\chi^2$ (13) | 78.68 | 86.65 | 173.15 | 174.52 | 168.73 | 176.55 |
| Prob > LR $\chi^2$ | 0.0000 | 0.0000 | 0.0000 | 0.0000 | 0.0000 | 0.0000 |
| Pseudo $R^2$ | –0.0246 | –0.2256 | –0.0917 | –0.1120 | –0.1105 | –0.0850 |

*Source*: Fifth Employment and Human Resource Development Research Organization (labour market working group) (March 2001) of the Japan Institute of Labour in the old Ministry of Labour

*Notes*: 1. The data used in this analysis were taken from the establishments studied in the *Employment Trend Survey* for 1996 as well as from supplementary material. These establishments were private sector workplaces with more than 500 employees. The dependent variable was the number of job openings for those expecting to graduate in March 1997. The date of the survey was as of the end of June 1996. Companies that at that time responded they were not hiring were put at zero; those that were undecided were omitted from the sample. The estimate method was the tobit model. The t-values are given in parentheses.

2. In addition to those given above, the explanatory variables include a constant, a metropolitan area dummy (either Tokyo, Osaka, Aichi, Kanagawa, or not), a company size dummy (100–999 or 1000 or more), as well as dummies for major industrial sectors; the impact of differences in region, company size and industry were not considered. Further details can be found in Genda Yūji, "Who Really Lost Jobs in Japan? Youth Employment in an Aging Japanese Society", *Labor Markets and Firm Benefit Policies in Japan and the United States,* eds. Ogura Seiritsu, Tachibanaki Toshiaki, and David Wise (Chicago: University of Chicago Press, 2003).

# *Chapter 3*

# *Misconceptions about Freeters*

## An evil government plot?

*Playboy Weekly* is a Japanese magazine that counts freeters as a main component of its readership. In November 2000 it published a special issue entitled, "Has a Government Witch-Hunt on Freeters Begun?" The magazine's contributors considered efforts by the then Education[1] and Labour ministries to eliminate freeters—whose existence the authorities had branded "disgraceful"—to be an evil government plot. Earlier that year in the 2000 *White Paper on Labour*, the government calculated that the number of freeters in 1997 was 1.51 million and attempted to look into the reasons why, in the five short years since 1992, the freeter population had increased by 500,000. The fact that the *White Paper* regarded this sudden increase as a problem was by no means an evil government plot; rather, it reflects a legitimate concern about the adverse effects on Japanese society and the Japanese economy were the number of freeters to rise and the trend to avoid becoming regular employees, with the heavy workplace demands that full-time status entails, to become widespread among Japanese youth. The *White Paper* introduced data showing that, by their late twenties, a growing number of young people, including

1. As a result of the reorganization of national government offices in 2001, the former Ministry of Education, Science and Culture is now the Ministry of Education, Culture, Sports, Science and Technology.

many who had chosen to become freeters immediately after graduation, hope to find full-time jobs; it went on to explain the importance of promoting suitable vocational choices for young people. Although the fact that the *White Paper* branded freeters "disgraceful" is problematic, for *Playboy Weekly* to jump to the conclusion that all government policies to deal with them are evil could probably itself be described as a form of labeling.

Unfortunately, however, the concerns of the government and of grownups anxious about the future of Japan do not reach the ears of most young people. Virtually all of them believe that being a freeter is a matter of free choice, and, generally speaking, they have a positive view of freeters. "Why should I make the effort to become a regular full-time employee," they ask, "since I am bound to lose my job through restructuring?" Or, if the young person has studied the situation a bit more carefully, he/she might conclude: "The reason adults are so worried about young people becoming freeters is because they are afraid that the public pension plan will go bankrupt." No matter how earnestly grownups prepare labour white papers or educational television specials on the subject, their concern never reaches the freeters themselves.

What is a freeter and why does a young person choose to become one? A Japanese neologism derived from the English word *free* and the German word *Arbeiter* (labourer), the word refers to young people who are not regularly employed but who work at one or more part-time jobs or at one short-term job after another. They have been classified into three types based on their reasons for becoming freeters: those who are "pursuing their dreams," those "taking a moratorium" until they discover what they really want to do, and those who "had no alternative." But the truth is that the vast majority probably became freeters without any clear intention of doing so; in the final analysis, even they don't know why they ended up as such. Rather than young people choosing to become freeters as the result of a clear and conscious individual decision, the choice has been made for them—without their even realizing what is happening—by the socio-economic system. At the root of this system are the various subsystems discussed in chapter 2 that give priority to middle-aged and older workers.

The job insecurities of middle-aged and older Japanese white collar workers are old news. But, as I have repeatedly said, of the more than three million unemployed, a mere 50,000 are college graduates between the ages of forty-five and fifty-four. As a trade-off for protecting the jobs of middle-aged and older workers, large companies with graying workforces are likely to cut back on the hiring of new graduates. The number of freeters has risen in direct proportion to the job opportunities offering high salaries and a chance for skill development that have been taken away from all but a handful of young people.

## The "seven-five-three" turnover rate

Invariably lurking behind any discussion be it of freeters or parasite singles are fears about a decline in the work ethic of Japanese young people. They also come under attack for what is known as the "seven-five-three" job turnover rate. The term refers to the percentage of recent graduates who quit their jobs within three years of employment—seventy percent in the case of junior high school graduates, fifty percent for high school graduates, and thirty percent for college graduates. These figures have a high degree of reliability since they are based on records of workers insured under the employment insurance system administered by the Ministry of Health, Labour and Welfare. "Lifetime employees"—those who, as the term implies, work for a single company from the time they graduate to the time they retire—have already become a rare phenomenon among Japanese youth.

Although the definition of freeter is not entirely clear, the word has come to symbolize "those who will not (or cannot) hold a steady job" or "who soon quit"; and, to be sure, the number of young people cut off from any chance for full-time, long-term employment has been steadily rising. On the other hand, however, many young people would like to become full-time employees. If anything, this latter trend has been growing even stronger. The *Employment Status Survey* conducted by the Statistics Bureau of the Management and Coordination Agency was used in figure 3-1 to determine how many of those planning to change jobs would like to become full-time employees. The percentages have been rising among both fifteen- to twenty-four-year-olds and twenty-

**Fig. 3-1 Percentage of Job Changers Who "Want to Work as a Regular Full-time Employee"**

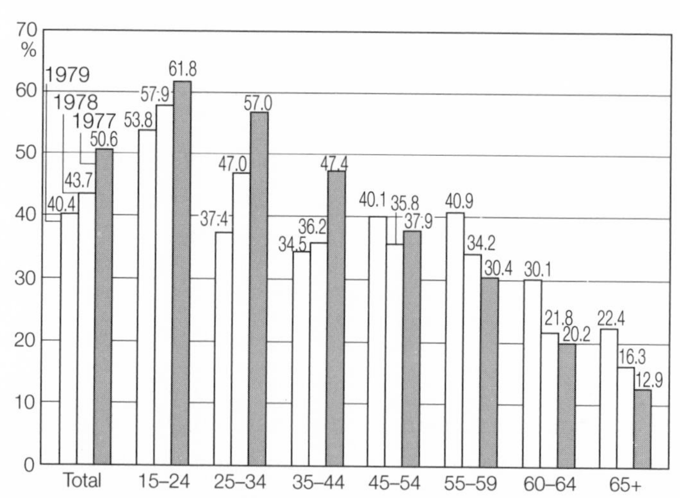


*Source*: Statistics Bureau, Management and Coordination Agency, *Employment Status Survey*.
*Note*: All figures and tables in chapter 3, including this one, are based on Genda Yūji and Kurosawa Masako, "Transition from School to Work in Japan," *Journal of the Japanese and International Economies* 15 (December 2001): 465-488.

five- to thirty-four year-olds. In fact, many of the young people who are changing jobs are doing so with the express hope of finding a more suitable full-time position.

Changes in recent graduates' attitudes toward work have been cited as the reason behind the trend away from regular full-time employment. But have attitudes among young graduates with no plans to go on to higher education in fact undergone such a radical change? As far as we can tell from statistical data, it is hard to believe that their work ethic has deteriorated significantly. The grounds for this conclusion can be found in figure 3-2. The *Survey of Young Employees* conducted by the Ministry of Health, Labour and Welfare breaks down, by year of graduation/school leaving, the reasons given for not becoming a full-time employee right after graduating from or leaving school. A glance at this figure shows no discernible trend to suggest that the percentage of those who responded that they "had no desire to work as a full-time employee" has risen since 1989. To be sure, the percentage rose temporarily

**Fig. 3-2 Reasons for Not Becoming a Full-time Employee Immediately after Graduating from (or Leaving) School** (Share)

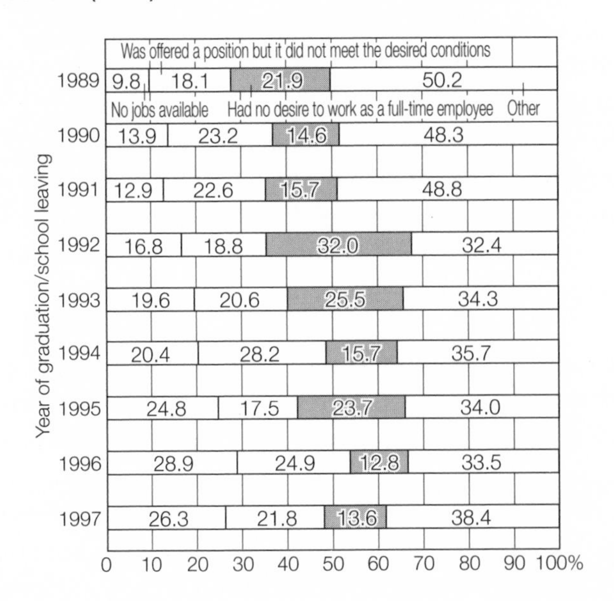


to thirty-one percent among those who graduated or left school in 1992. At that time it was still possible for young people to believe that their difficulties in finding a job would be short lived, that economic conditions would soon improve, and that if they just became freeters and waited it out, they would find a position they wanted. Since then, however, as the recession has lengthened, most young people are aware that not only does becoming a freeter reduce their chances of finding a job they want, it makes it even more difficult to get any regular full-time work at all. As a result, there has been no perceptible upward trend in the percentage who say they do not want to be full-time employees: only 13.6 percent of those who graduated in 1997 gave this response.

Nor can any trend be found in the percentage who responded that they had not taken a full-time job because it "did not meet the desired conditions," a response which serves as a proxy indicator for young people's commitment to work. That percentage has not increased significantly since the beginning of the 1990s, except for those who graduated or left school in 1994 when it rose to 28.2 percent. The rate for all other years has been in the high teens or low twenties. The younger generation's commitment to work cannot be said to be weakening. On the other hand, a steady rise can be found in the percentage of those who responded there were "no jobs available." Only 9.8 percent of the cohort that graduated or left school in 1989 gave this response; for the 1994 cohort the response rate was more than twenty percent, and for graduates from 1996 on it has risen to the high twenties. Thus a more important reason for young people's failure to become regular full-time employees is not a structural change in their work ethic but rather a change in the environment—i.e., a decline in employment opportunities that would allow them to put their talents to use at full-time jobs.

I do not mean to imply, of course, that all young people want full-time work. If a person who did not become a full-time employee upon graduation decides not to become one later on, undoubtedly one reason is that he/she "has no desire to work as a full-time employee." There are, however, two factors that have a far greater impact on youth employment than a reputed change in attitudes and that affect both the transition from school to work and the likelihood that an individual, once hired, will remain at a job, namely, (1) the unique structure of the Japanese employment market and (2) vocational guidance at schools.

## The labour market's "cohort effect"

If no clear deterioration in young people's work ethic can be discerned, then how do we account for the "seven-five-three" phenomenon among recent graduates? The reason is undeniable: a worsening labour market environment.

It is common knowledge that when market demand for recent graduates deteriorates, the chances are limited that they will be hired as regular full-time employees. But the market's impact on their future working life is not confined to how easy or difficult it may be to get hired. Even among those who became full-time employees immediately after graduation, the higher the unemployment rate in the year before graduation the stronger their tendency to quit later on. Simply put, students who graduate during a recession are more likely to adhere to the "seven-five-three" pattern and subsequently change jobs. Why? Because a high unemployment rate inevitably means fewer job opportunities. As a result, it becomes harder and harder for recent graduates to find a job that fits their own individual skills and value systems. Most cannot get jobs at the company that is their first choice—or their second or third choice, for that matter, and so on down the line. Because they have reluctantly ended up at a company quite different from the one they hoped for, any minor dissatisfaction or trouble makes it easy to decide to change jobs. In economics this is called a "mismatch."

Since the collapse of the bubble economy in the 1990s, companies, primarily large ones, have been cutting back on the hiring of recent graduates. This prolonged and broad-based freeze on recruitment has greatly reduced the number of attractive employment opportunities at popular or well-known firms. Moreover, given the likelihood of low economic growth, the opportunity to work for a company with a promising future has also declined. In both cases the result has been to decrease the probability that a recent graduate will be offered a job where he/she would like to work and, consequently, to increase the tendency to leave a workplace chosen by default.

Job churning among young people and the rising number of freeters both raise the question of labour market mobility and diversification in types of employment. Why is it necessary for young people to settle down and become full-time employees in the first place? The answer has to do with improving vocational skills. From that perspective, it would appear to be useful, as matters now stand, either to work uninterruptedly as a regular employee or, if that is not possible, to have had at least once the experience of being one. The reason is seen in table 3-1, which shows that young people who find full-time positions after graduation and remain at their jobs have a higher incentive to improve their vocational skills. Conversely, among those who have never had any experience working as a full-time employee, only slightly more than half feel the need to do so. If having a high incentive to improve one's own skills is indispensable for increasing productivity, then there is no question of the importance of providing an environment which enables a young person to concentrate on his/her work.

**Table 3-1 Relation between Employment Experience and the Desire to Acquire or Improve One's Vocational Skills (Percent)**

| | Do you feel any need to acquire or improve your vocational skills? | | |
|---|---|---|---|
| | Yes | No | Don't know |
| Became a full-time employee immediately after graduation (83.8%) | 76.9 | 4.3 | 18.8 |
| Remained at company (59.8%) | 78.5 | 4.1 | 17.4 |
| Changed jobs (23.8 %) | 73.0 | 4.6 | 22.4 |
| Did not become a full-time employee immediately after graduation (16.2%) | 66.9 | 5.8 | 27.3 |
| Had experience as a full-time employee (10.7%) | 72.2 | 4.7 | 23.1 |
| Had no experience as a full-time employee (5.4%) | 55.6 | 8.0 | 36.1 |

*Note*: Figures in parentheses are shares.

If the recession continues to make it difficult for young people to find full-time employment, however, it is inevitable that the percentage of vocational mismatches will continue to rise. If that happens, more and more young people will be driven to quit their jobs and look for new ones, and, as a result, an increasing number of young people may lose the incentive to develop their job skills. Until recently companies have had the principal role in skill development. But given the ever-growing trend to reduce personnel expenditures, it is becoming difficult for them to meet the cost of training. Increasingly, individual workers are being called upon to develop their own skills. If both companies and workers adopt a passive attitude toward skill development, in the long run this will lead to a decline in the productivity of Japanese society as a whole.

The decision to become a full-time employee at a particular company and remaining there is, of course, largely a personal one. And as such, it is neither possible, nor desirable, to compel someone to do so. On the other hand, an individual's innate attitudes and sense of values are not the only factors that influence that person's decision. It is not just a matter of work ethic; we must not forget that another determining factor is the demand environment of the labour market at the time a young person graduates from school. The calculations in figure 3-3 show how the number of times a person is a full-time employee during his/her teens and twenties fluctuates when there is a one percent rise in the unemployment rate in the year before graduating from or leaving school. As this figure indicates, a one percent rise in the unemployment rate during the year before graduation decreases the probability of working at least once as a full-time employee before the age of thirty by 7.3 points for males and 12.3 points for females. On the other hand, it raises the probability of not even once becoming a regular employee by 9.6 points for females and by 3.8 points for males. It also increases the probability of being a full-time employee at two or more companies as the result of a job change by 2.8 points and 3.4 points, respectively. A rise in the unemployment rate at the time of graduation not only makes it more difficult to find a full-time job, it also makes it virtually impossible to find the job one had hoped for. This in turn increases the tendency to quit and look for another one.

The state of the job market at the time of graduation not only affects where one works immediately after graduation but whether one subsequently remains there, and so consequently it has a lasting effect even on the remuneration one receives. The Japanese labour market is formed on a hiring model that is centered almost exclusively on recent graduates;

**Fig. 3-3 Marginal Effect on the Number of Times a Person under 30 Has Had the Experience of Being a Full-Time Employee When There Is a 1 Percent Rise in the Unemployment Rate in the Year before Graduating from (or Leaving)**

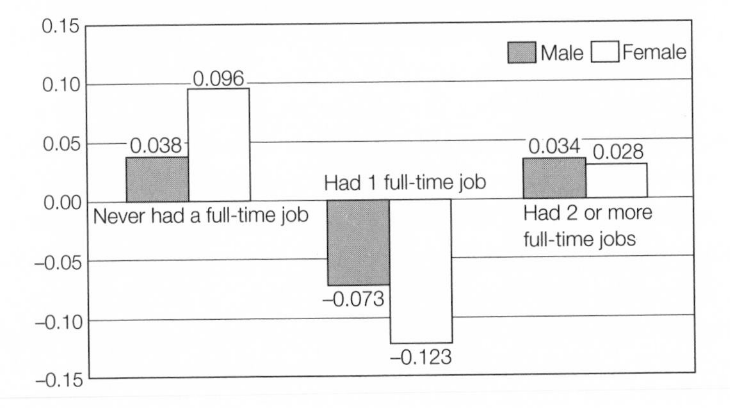

in short, the opportunity for choosing employment is concentrated on new graduates, and those opportunities diminish with age. As a result, the period immediately following graduation is not just the biggest, it is also the only opportunity a young person has to find a suitable job for the rest of his/her life. A person who loses this opportunity will find it quite difficult later on to get a job that will give him/her any sense of satisfaction. It is, quite literally, a worker's one and only chance. Under these circumstances the job market choices made at graduation or immediately thereafter greatly affect the formation of a person's lifetime career.

The year in which a person graduates and begins to work differs from cohort to cohort. A cohort that is fortunate enough to graduate during a period of economic prosperity will have a relatively easy time thereafter finding job opportunities. On the other hand, a cohort that has to look for work during a recession will find it quite difficult even in the future to get a satisfying job. This difference in working environment for each cohort is called the labour market's "cohort effect." It is precisely because of this cohort effect that the difficulties young people have in finding jobs is not just a problem when they are young but—though I am overstating it somewhat—remains so for the rest of their lives.

Traditionally, seniority-based wages, long-term employment, and company unions have all been cited as special characteristics of the way Japanese work. But in fact what lies behind all of these and most powerfully characterizes the true state of affairs in Japan is the existence of the cohort effect. If I were to define that effect somewhat more precisely, it refers to significant differences in wages and employment conditions that exist for each cohort, which in turn is classified by the year in which its constituents were born or by their last year of schooling. In Japan cohorts who graduate when the job market is favorable are most likely to receive higher wages later on. They are also most likely to be blessed with the opportunity for long-term employment. Also implicit in the cohort effect is the idea that because good jobs are scarce, a cohort with a large population will find long-term employment opportunities or high wages hard to come by.

If we think about the background against which the cohort effect traditionally functions in Japan (although its impact today has been severely circumscribed in order to protect the jobs of middle-aged and older workers), it is a unique form of employment management in which recruitment is basically concentrated on recent graduates, who are subsequently divided into cohorts and receive promotion, advancement, and other forms of treatment accordingly. There are still many members of the second baby boom generation, particularly college graduates, who passed through the deep freeze on hiring known as the "ultra ice age" right after the collapse of the bubble economy and have yet to find suitable jobs. Moreover, because of the size of that cohort, those who do have jobs face difficulties being promoted that their parents' generation never encountered. We must not forget the possibility that the cohort of graduates hired after the collapse of the bubble economy, primarily the second baby boom generation, have been placed in a harsh situation unlike anything ever experienced by previous cohorts.

## Vocational guidance at the crossroads

Another reason recent graduates do not stay on as full-time employees has to do with the vocational guidance system and the way advice is given at schools.

In a job market dubbed the "ice age" vocational guidance now stands at a crossroads. The customary approach has been the "one person, one company" system: a high school singles out a company and introduces it as a prospective place of employment to a student who is looking for a job. The system is now under review as a result of mounting criticism about the way a school makes its selections: even when it takes a student's wishes into account, its decision is ultimately based on its own assessment of his/her skills and aptitude. The "Summary of the Interim Report of the Committee Studying the Employment Problems of High School Students" published by the Ministry of Education (August 2000) cited the need to limit as much as possible the way guidance, introductions, and placement services are carried out under the "one person, one company" system. It also called on each school to respect its students' wishes and to make sure that the selection it makes on their behalf is really suited to their aptitudes and skills.

On the other hand, it is also true that recommendations from teachers and the vocational guidance given at schools play a key role in helping students to settle into full-time jobs. Many schools and high school teachers make enormous efforts to smooth the way for their students and secure positions for them even in an adverse employment environment. In addition to their teaching duties, quite a few teachers give up their free time to provide advice and counseling about finding a job. One result of this vocational guidance system and the steady stream of students it introduces to potential employers is the relationship of trust that has been forged between companies and schools, a relationship that makes for superb matches no third party could possibly hope to achieve. Teachers know that "such-and-such a student of ours may not have good grades, but he/she is sure to please the head of X Company. Their personalities match, and the student will get good training there. That is likely to be the best place for him/her."

But as an increasing number of companies that once used to provide employment for students under this system post poor results, go bankrupt, or move production offshore, this ongoing exchange between schools and companies is likely to come to a total standstill. As it becomes ever more difficult for schools to acquire adequate information about places of employment, it is harder and harder for them to give vocational guidance or recommend positions that will correspond to their students' aptitudes. As a result, mismatches are more likely to occur, causing some to decide to become freeters and eventually increasing the probability that even those who manage to become full-time employees will quit their jobs.

Has vocational guidance at schools already lost its effectiveness? Figure 3-4 shows the percentage of young people who became full-time employees immediately after graduating from (or leaving) high school and who believe that the vocational guidance they received at school was useful. When the response given was "not useful" or "did not become a full-time employee" after graduation, it can be assumed that vocational guidance was not effective. When these latter two categories are combined, the percentage exceeds fifty percent for all years. If effective vocational guidance means increasing the likelihood of becoming a full-time employee, it has certainly failed to do so for a majority of high school graduates looking for work.

But there is another important fact that we can deduce from figure 3-4: among those who became full-time employees after graduation, the percentage who said that vocational guidance had not been useful is declining, as is the percentage of those who said they "did not receive vocational guidance." On the other hand, the percentage of those who responded that vocational guidance had been "useful" or "very useful" has been steadily rising since 1989/1990. In periods of labour shortages it used to be possible to find a full-time position even without any effective vocational guidance. But for cohorts that graduate in periods when jobs are scarce, the lack of useful vocational guidance at school reinforces the tendency not to find full-time work. During a recession, when it is difficult to find a position suited to one's skills and temperament and

**Fig. 3-4 Was Vocational Guidance at School Useful for Finding a Full-time Position Immediately after Graduation from High School?**

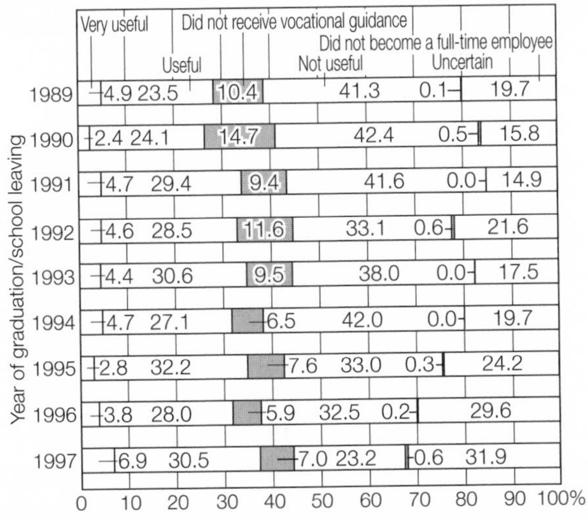


*Note*: Figures given are percentages of all graduates, including those who did not become full-time employees immediately after graduating from (or leaving) high school. Except in the case of those "who did not a become full-time employee," the values are for high school graduates (general track or vocational track) who became full-time employees right after graduation.

hard to obtain adequate information about prospective places of employment, students' expectations about their school's vocational guidance tend to go up.

## Are freeters really the problem?

Freeters have no desire to become regular full-time employees and are content to work part-time or do side jobs, or, if such jobs are not available, they choose not to work at all. They repeat the pattern of finding a job, quitting shortly later, then moving on to a new one. They have a weak sense of self-reliance and are economically dependent on their parents. They want to distance themselves from the workplace environment and sometimes from society itself. To account for the growing number of young freeters, critics have cited a change in their work ethic and, especially, a diminished sense of purpose. But despite all the talk about a change in attitudes toward work, drawing a distinction between the innate attitudes of an individual and the impact that the surrounding environment may have on him/her is not so simple.

There are people who do their job—and even work overtime and on their days off—without ever managing to finish everything they have to do. Some may think that theirs is a voluntary choice: that they love their work and do it because they want to. But if we were to look at the situation from the perspective of the individuals themselves, it is by no means a matter of doing so because they want to. It is not even a matter of doing so for the sake of future advancement. They simply have to or risk inconveniencing clients or customers by failing to get their work done on time. All the more so when staff has been cut back and individual workloads increase.

Just as it is hard to determine whether work is voluntary or involuntary, much the same could be said of freeters. It may come as a surprise, but among those who looked for work during the "ultra ice age" of the early 1990s when the unemployment rate was particularly high, even the ones who became full-time employees had a strong tendency to quit their jobs. Though they persevered and against all odds found full-time positions, they tended to become freeters in the long run. Why? Because when economic conditions are bad, it is difficult to find suitable employment opportunities since the number of jobs themselves are scarce. The probability was low for the members of the cohort that did find jobs during the "ultra ice age" that these jobs really suited them. As a result, the number of "voluntary" job turnovers subsequently increased. A lack of demand in society as a whole led to such mismatches.

Although the tendency is to lump them all together, individuals have different reasons for becoming freeters. According to the 2000 *White Paper on Labour*, twenty-five percent have definite objectives for the future; only a mere seven percent find any value per se in being freeters and wish to continue as such. The remaining seventy percent became freeters because they feel uneasy about the future or for other reasons. But if it were truly a matter of attitudes, the most honest answer to the question "Why did you become a freeter?" would probably be: "I have no idea." It is not as if they had any clear intention of doing so; it is not even as if they hold society to blame because they cannot find a full-time job.

Being a freeter is a phenomenon that affects some but not all young people. And so isn't it important not to exaggerate the issue out of all proportion? On the other hand, a growing number of young people during the recession have been working excessively long hours, as we shall see in greater detail in chapter 5. It is unjust to regard this as not being a problem at all. The number of young people under the age of thirty-five who work more than sixty hours a week and more than 200 days a year has soared to 1.9 million (*Employment Status Survey* for 1999). Calculated on the basis of a two-day weekend system, this means that the number of young people who work every day from nine in the morning until after ten o'clock at night with an hour's break squeezed in is far in excess of the 1.5 million who are freeters. Yet the long hours of work are not thought to be a problem; one hardly ever hears the concern raised that this may be the cause of late marriages among Japanese young people.

In thinking about youth employment it is important to avoid labeling. Economic affluence has led to diversification in the options available to the young; hence, becoming a freeter may seem to be the product of free choice. On the other hand, however, the Japanese labour market is imperceptibly moving in the direction of a two-tiered system in which a small percentage of young people find satisfying jobs whereas the vast majority do not. In the case of the freeter phenomenon, there has been too much emphasis on the need for change: the tone of the argument has been that freeters ought to mend their ways. But if the tendency to use that argument increases, it will probably make the situation even more dangerous. And it is not just freeters; young people who withdraw from social contact and lock themselves up at home have also become a topic of popular concern in Japan. Young people who are slow to establish a proper distance between themselves and society are and always have been a deviation from the norm. Only the names used to describe them change: moratorium people; stay-at-homes; capsule people. Each generation frets about the one that comes next and that it finds strange and incomprehensible.

When adults brand young people as having an inadequate work ethic and try to reform them, the pent-up discontent of the young is likely to explode. Agitators will begin to appear and take advantage of this discontent causing needless social confusion. Or am I perhaps being overly pessimistic?

## The data speak

### Behind the "seven-five-three" phenomenon

Why do young people who have become full-time employees quit their jobs? It is possible to analyze the reasons in detail. The data used are taken from the *Survey of Young Employees,* which the then Ministry of Labour conducted in July 1997. This survey studied approximately 12,000 private sector workplaces with five or more full-time employees and a random sampling of 21,000 young people below the age of thirty employed by them. The focus here was on "employees' recall data" to generate work histories since graduation; employment conditions and the work ethic of the young people themselves were also surveyed.

Not included in this survey of young graduates (or, to be more precise, those who graduated from or left school) were those who were out of the labour force or unemployed or who were working in the public sector or at workplaces with fewer than five employees. According to the *Employment Status Survey* conducted in 1997 by the then Management and Coordination Agency, 67.8 percent of all workers between the ages of fifteen and twenty-nine worked at private sector workplaces with five or more employees. Thus the analysis that follows takes into account around seventy percent of all Japanese young people.

Table 3-2 encapsulates the employment experience of the workers under thirty who were studied. A glance shows that, although the number of freeters is said to be on the rise, in fact, more than eighty percent of those surveyed became full-time employees immediately after graduation. As of 1997 sixty percent of them were still working full-time at the same firm. Of the approximately ten million who had become full-time employees, nearly three million had at some time changed jobs.

On the other hand, of the two million who did not find a full-time job after graduation, more than 1.3 million subsequently found full-time employment of one kind or other. Among those who quit their jobs, most of those who had become full-time employees after graduation, as well as most of those who did not, changed jobs at least once and had the experience of working full-time for two companies. Five percent, or

**Table 3-2 Employment Experiences of Workers Aged 15-29 Employed in Private Sector Workplaces with 5 or More Employees** (Figures weighted to restore share in the population)

| | Estimated numbers (10,000 persons) | Share (%) |
|---|---|---|
| (1) Entire population[1] | 1233.7 | 100.0 |
| (2) Became a full-time employee upon leaving school | 1033.3 | 83.8 |
| (2.1) Never changed employers | 737.4 | 59.8 |
| (2.2) Changed employers | 293.7 | 23.8 |
| (2.2.1) Had 1 full-time job | 85.5 | 6.9 |
| (2.2.2) Had 2 different full-time jobs | 132.6 | 10.8 |
| (2.2.3) Had 3 different full-time jobs | 40.3 | 3.3 |
| (2.2.4) Had 4 or more different full-time jobs | 14.7 | 1.2 |
| (3) Did not become a full-time employee upon leaving school | 200.3 | 16.2 |
| Reasons for not becoming a full-time employee Couldn't find a full-time job | 37.6 | 3.1 |
| Didn't take a full-time job, although such jobs were available | 42.7 | 3.5 |
| Didn't want to take a full-time job in the first place | 40.8 | 3.3 |
| Other | 76.5 | 6.2 |
| (3.1) Found a full-time job | 132.4 | 10.7 |
| (3.1.1) Never changed employers[2] | 36.2 | 2.9 |
| (3.1.2) Changed employers | 86.8 | 7.0 |
| (3.1.2.1) Still employed at first full-time job | 31.4 | 2.5 |
| (3.1.2.2) No longer employed at first full-time job | 54.1 | 4.4 |
| (3.1.2.2.1) Had 1 full-time job | 17.5 | 1.4 |
| (3.1.2.2.2) Had 2 full-time jobs | 24.8 | 2.0 |
| (3.1.2.2.3) Had 3 full-time jobs | 8.9 | 0.7 |
| (3.1.2.2.4) Had 4 or more full-time jobs | 2.4 | 0.2 |
| (3.2) Never had a full-time job | 66.3 | 5.4 |
| Major activities since leaving school | | |
| (3.2.1) Looking for a job | 3.2 | 0.3 |
| (3.2.2) Part-time work | 42.4 | 3.4 |
| (3.2.3) Domestic help | 4.0 | 0.3 |
| (3.2.4) Studying to acquire qualifications or skills | 6.0 | 0.5 |
| (3.2.5) Community service/volunteer work | 0.0 | 0.0 |
| (3.2.6) Hobby | 2.2 | 0.2 |
| (3.2.7) Other activities | 8.0 | 0.7 |

*Notes*: 1. Excludes youth who are unemployed or out of the labour force or are working either in the public sector or at firms with fewer than 5 regular workers, as well as those who are still in school.

2. Workers originally employed as non-regular employees who later became full-time employees at the firm.

660,000, had never once been a full-time employee. Most of these cited part-time work or side jobs as their main activity. (In some instances the totals do not add up because some questions received no response.)

What factors contributed to the likelihood that those who had become full-time employees after graduation would subsequently leave their jobs? Indicators for the quality of vocational matching as well as for the time spent working at the company where a graduate first became a full-time employee were considered in analyzing determinants of length of tenure. The higher the degree of satisfaction with the job, the higher the probability that an individual would continue to work at that company. The first factor considered was the unemployment rate in the year before graduation. If the unemployment rate is high during the period of job search, i.e., the year before graduation, not only is finding a full-time job difficult, even when the search is successful, the job may not necessarily be a satisfying one. In that case, the higher the unemployment rate, the more likely it is that the match will not work and that this in turn will increase the probability of quitting.

If the unemployment rate at the time of graduation is high and a young person is unable either to find a job he/she likes or to work for the company of his/her choice, the probability is also high that he/she will subsequently quit and look for a more satisfying position once the unemployment rate goes down and the economy expands again. In that case, the unemployment rate not only in the year before graduation but also in the years following employment needs to be considered. Table 3-3 gives the estimated results for both sexes and for males and females separately. These figures express the likelihood of job separation: of quitting the company one was employed at after graduation and looking for a new job. For instance, the coefficient of the unemployment rate in the year prior to graduating is 0.318 for both sexes, 0.363 for men only, and 0.322 for women only, all of which are positive numbers. This means that a rise in the unemployment rate in the year before graduation encourages quitting, i.e., makes it more likely that a recent graduate will leave the company where he/she is employed. The p-value here is an indicator of the model's statistical validity; a value below 0.05 is thought to be statistically meaningful. Since the p-values for the

**Table 3-3 Determinants of the Probability That Those Who Became Full-time Employees Immediately after Graduating from (or Leaving) School Will Quit Their First Regular Full-time Job** (Proportional hazard model: 15–29 years old)

| | Total | | Male | | Female | |
|---|---|---|---|---|---|---|
| | Coefficient | P-value | Coefficient | P-value | Coefficient | P-value |
| Unemployment rate after being employed | –0.085 | 0.00 | –0.221 | 0.01 | –0.050 | 0.41 |
| Unemployment rate in the year prior to leaving school | 0.318 | 0.00 | 0.363 | 0.00 | 0.322 | 0.00 |
| Main advisor in selecting the job (own decision)* | | | | | | |
| School teachers or alumni | –0.119 | 0.00 | –0.115 | 0.06 | –0.125 | 0.00 |
| Parents | –0.205 | 0.00 | –0.146 | 0.11 | –0.240 | 0.00 |
| Siblings, relatives, or friends | –0.004 | 0.95 | 0.150 | 0.20 | –0.071 | 0.37 |
| Public employment office | 0.080 | 0.57 | –0.115 | 0.66 | 0.273 | 0.10 |
| Others | 0.266 | 0.00 | 0.233 | 0.10 | 0.269 | 0.01 |
| Vocational guidance at school (was not useful)* | | | | | | |
| Was useful | –0.280 | 0.00 | –0.384 | 0.00 | –0.250 | 0.00 |
| Didn't receive vocational guidance or wasn't available at school | –0.144 | 0.00 | –0.079 | 0.25 | –0.176 | 0.00 |
| Trend term | | | | | | |
| Sample size | 16,393 | | 7,501 | | 8,892 | |
| LR $\chi^2$ (d.f.) | 2548.14 (37) | | 1087.71 (36) | | 955.85 (36) | |
| Log likelihood | –48497.04 | | –13648.55 | | –31348.98 | |

*Notes*: 1. Items in parentheses and marked with an asterisk are standards of comparison, i.e., reference groups. For example, in the case of recommendations from teachers or alumni at one's school, the result –0.119 (the total for both sexes) means that such recommendations made it more difficult to quit later on than if the student had chosen the company him/herself.

2. In addition to those given above, such factors as "gender," "level of education," "most important criterion in selecting the job," and "occupation at first regular full-time job" also served as explanatory variables. For further discussion see Kurosawa and Genda Yūji, "Transition from School to Work in Japan," *Journal of the Japanese and International Economies* 15 (December 2001): 465–488.

3. The LR $\chi^2$ and log likelihood are both indicators measuring the soundness of the estimated results.

unemployment rate in the year before graduation are all zero, it undoubtedly affects the probability of quitting.

Conversely, the coefficient of the unemployment rate for the years after becoming a full-time employee was negative, minus 0.085, for both sexes. This means that a rise in the unemployment rate after employment inhibits the probability of quitting; in other words, it makes it more difficult to quit. In the case of both sexes and of males only, the effect was statistically significant. These results reflect the fact that if the unemployment rate rises after a graduate has found a job, he/she tends to avoid changing employers because job hunting has become more difficult. When the unemployment rate is high while someone is looking for a job and before joining a company, however, that person is apt to decide later on to change jobs because his/her work is not satisfying. This can be statistically confirmed.

One other important factor has an effect on the probability of quitting one's job: vocational guidance and recommendations given at school. The coefficient is negative not only in the case of recommendations from parents but also when a student chooses a place of employment on the basis of recommendations from a teacher or an alumnus/a. In short, a recommendation from one's school makes it difficult to quit the company where one is employed and reinforces the tendency to remain there.

Moreover, the coefficient for respondents who answered yes to the question "Was vocational guidance at school useful when you were looking for a job?" was minus 0.280 for both sexes, and the p-value was zero. Those who felt that vocational guidance had been useful found it more difficult to quit later on than those who did not. From this it can be inferred that the vocational guidance a student receives at the time of choosing a place of employment contributes to the probability of remaining at the company chosen. Vocational guidance is particularly effective in the case of males.

For those interested in learning more about the findings of this empirical analysis, please refer to "Transition from School to Work in Japan," an article I co-authored with Kurosawa Masako and published in the *Journal of the Japanese and International Economies* (December 2001). It

Sanwa Research Institute's *Comprehensive Survey of Youth Employment and Unemployment* (Employment and Human Resource Development Organization of Japan, 2000).

# *Chapter 4*

# *Averting a Clash of Generations*

## Reservations about abolishing mandatory retirement

From an economic perspective "discrimination" refers to a situation in which people who have the same skills and make the same amount of effort are compensated or evaluated differently for reasons over which they have no control. Clear differences in income, employment opportunities, and the like among persons of different gender, race, or nationality inevitably raise the specter of discrimination which cannot be overlooked.

Japanese workers who are approaching their sixtieth birthday face an obstacle that does not affect their younger counterparts: the mandatory retirement system. Age-related discrimination is prohibited by law in the United States, and mandatory retirement does not exist there. In Japan too more and more people are beginning to feel that mandatory retirement is a form of discrimination based on age. One reason for the mounting misgivings about the mandatory retirement system is the contention that Japan will need to make full use of the talents of its senior citizens. Since the percentage of the elderly is expected to increase significantly, it is likely that a growing number of workers will want to continue working even after they reach the age of sixty. The recent decision to raise the pensionable age will also make it difficult for many older people to maintain stable incomes while they are in their early sixties.

To avoid such problems when that time comes, the government is searching for ways to make it possible for workers to continue working until the age of sixty-five. A few years from now when the Japanese labour force population will have reached its peak and begins to decline, it is reasonable to assume that older people will be encouraged to work in order to maintain a sufficient labour supply. One special feature of the Japanese labour market not found in other advanced industrialized countries is the high unemployment rate among seniors. Inevitably this has led to strong demands that they be given access to reliable employment opportunities. These demands have come not only from labour unions, which protect the rights of workers, but also from researchers who have the public interest in mind (see, for example, Seike Atsushi, *Teinen Hatan* [The Breakdown of Mandatory Retirement], [Tokyo: Kōdansha, 2000]).

Beginning in the year 2007, the first baby boom generation (those born primarily between 1947 and 1949) will start to face mandatory retirement under the current system. As that time approaches, the view is likely to gain support that Japan should ban age-related discrimination and abolish the mandatory retirement system altogether. Such steps would be justifiable on the grounds that treating people differently because of their age should be regarded as discrimination. The position could even be taken that the mandatory retirement system violates a basic human rights of older people, their right to work.

But we also need to recognize that raising the official mandatory retirement age from sixty to sixty-five is very likely to entail some adverse consequences. At present most companies have no intention of changing the current system. In fact, according to the 2000 *Survey of Employment Management* conducted by the then Ministry of Labour, ninety-three percent of companies that have a fixed-age mandatory retirement system say they have "no plans to change." The situation is entirely different from the one that prevailed at the time when the Equal Opportunity law was enacted; instead of targeting a few firms allegedly engaged in gender-based discrimination, changes are now being called for in a system supported by the vast majority of Japanese companies.

Though raising the retirement age or abolishing the system altogether may protect the jobs of those who are already employed, the serious concern is that it will take job opportunities away from those who are trying to enter the labour market. In short, protecting the employment opportunities of older workers is likely to cause a significant reduction in the hiring of young people. Up until the end of the bubble economy in the early 1990s the claim used to be made that there would always be jobs for young people because of an ongoing labour shortage. Such opinions are rarely heard now that youth unemployment has risen to unprecedented heights and is becoming a serious problem.

The counterargument could be made that, when asked, quite a few companies which have already raised the retirement age or are considering doing so respond that "revision of the retirement system does not necessarily reduce the hiring of new graduates." In fact, some personnel managers even go so far as to claim that recruitment and the raising of the retirement age are two entirely separate issues. But is that really the case?

## The current state of the mandatory retirement system

Using the *Survey of Employment Management*, which the Ministry of Health, Labour and Welfare conducts every year, let us first try to take an in-depth look at the current state of efforts to raise the retirement age at companies with thirty or more employees.

In tandem with its plans to raise the age at which citizens can begin collecting public pensions, the Japanese government is also working on ways to extend employment into the early sixties. As table 4-1 shows, however, nearly eighty percent of all companies have a system of mandatory retirement at age sixty, and, what is more, they have no intention of changing it. This percentage rises with the size of the company. The remaining twenty percent can be broken down into four categories: (1) companies that have already adopted a mandatory retirement system that applies to all workers at age sixty-one or older; (2) those that have mandatory retirement at age sixty but have decided to raise it or are considering doing so; (3) those that do not have a mandatory retirement system; and (4) those that have a mandatory retirement system based on job category rather than age.

**Table 4-1 Present State of Retirement Systems** (Share of companies, %)

| Present state of retirement systems | Number of regular full-time employees | | | | |
|---|---|---|---|---|---|
| | 1,000 or more | 300–999 | 100–299 | 30–99 | Total |
| Has a mandatory retirement system for all workers at age 61 or older | 3.4 | 3.3 | 6.0 | 7.8 | 7.0 |
| At present has a mandatory retirement system for all workers at age 60, but has decided to raise the age limit to 61 or older or is considering doing so | 2.6 | 3.4 | 2.6 | 4.5 | 4.0 |
| Has no mandatory retirement system | 0.1 | 0.4 | 1.6 | 12.2 | 9.0 |
| Has a retirement system based on job category | 1.7 | 2.5 | 1.2 | 1.6 | 1.5 |
| Has a mandatory retirement system for all workers at age 60 and no plans to change | 92.2 | 90.5 | 88.7 | 73.9 | 78.4 |

*Data*: 2000 *Survey of Employment Management*
*Source*: "Millennium Project: Research Report on Measures to Promote Continued Employment into the Early Sixties" (interim report) prepared by the Association of Employment Development for Senior Citizens, commissioned in fiscal year 2001 by the Ministry of Health, Labour and Welfare. All tables and figures in chapter 4, including this one, have been taken from this report.

Furthermore, companies that have already adopted a system of retirement at age sixty-one or older give different reasons for extending the retirement age than those that have decided to make such a move or are considering doing so. A glance at table 4-2 shows that a high percentage of the former cite "make use of workers' skills and experience," whereas the latter tend to cite "build a system to deal with the eventual rise in the public pension eligibility age" and the "demands of society." This latter type of company can afford to make efficient use of their older employees and is able to cope with changes in the external environment, such as revisions to the social insurance system.

On the other hand, as figure 4-1 shows, companies that have mandatory retirement at age sixty are more likely than ones with a retirement age of sixty-one or older to have problems related to personnel evaluations. The gap is particularly great among those who responded that their "evaluators' training is inadequate"; the response rate was 50.8 per-

**Table 4-2 Reasons for Raising the Retirement Age to 61 or Over**
**(Multiple responses, %)**

| Reasons | Companies that have already raised the retirement age | Companies that have decided to raise the retirement age or are considering doing so | Total |
|---|---|---|---|
| Make use of workers' skills and experience | 59.5 | 48.0 | 55.3 |
| Improve workplace morale | 7.9 | 8.5 | 8.1 |
| Union demands | 4.7 | 7.0 | 5.6 |
| Able to reduce personnel costs because such workers receive public pensions | 16.2 | 23.1 | 18.7 |
| Build a system to deal with the eventual rise in the public pension eligibility age | 18.6 | 54.9 | 31.8 |
| Demands of society | 29.6 | 42.9 | 34.4 |
| Other | 10.4 | 6.3 | 8.9 |

*Data*: 2000 *Survey of Employment Management*

cent, nearly double that for companies with a retirement age of sixty-one or older (26.8 percent). Similarly, those that responded that their "evaluation criteria are unclear or not standardized" was 42.3 percent among the former but only 21.5 percent among the latter. These findings suggest that many companies regard raising the retirement age as problematic because their personnel departments do not have the evaluation criteria needed to provide individualized supervision. If all companies felt their evaluators' training was adequately conducted and their evaluation standards clear, then raising the retirement age might be welcome, but this is obviously only an ideal. There is hardly any company that does not have problems with its personnel evaluation system.

Moreover, if the mandatory retirement age is to be raised or the system abolished altogether, there will be an increasing need to introduce a specialist system. (For a more detailed discussion see "The data speak" at the end of the chapter.) Its antithesis is an ability-based grade system which forms the basis of most existing personnel systems. Companies with mandatory retirement at age sixty have an ability-based grade sys-

**Fig. 4-1 Problems with the Personnel Evaluation System or the Way It Operates** (Multiple responses)

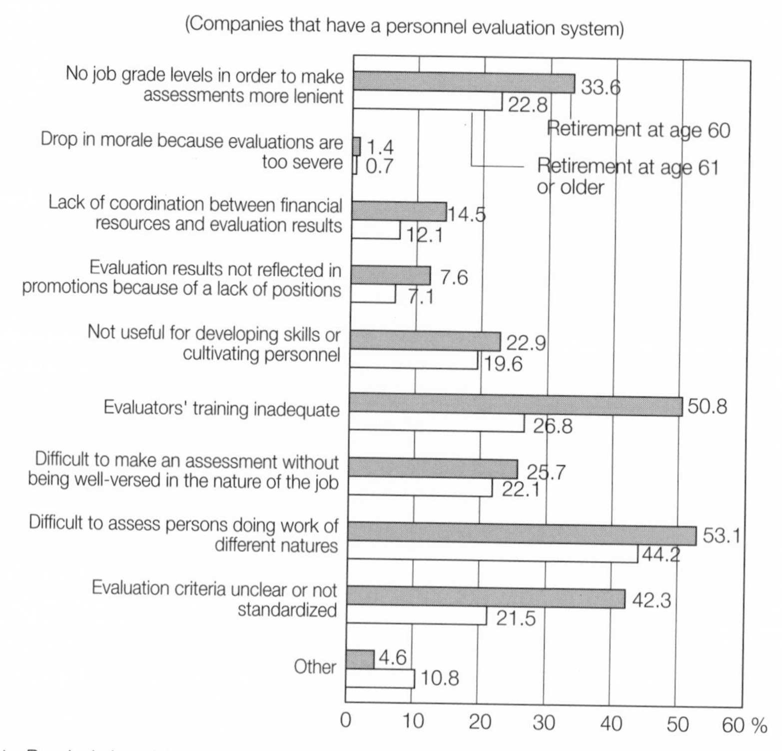


*Data*: Recalculation of the 1998 *Survey of Employment Management*

tem and basically intend to keep on using it. This system sets several levels of competency based on job performance, knowledge and skills, and experience, then rates each employee on his/her competency in each area, and makes these ratings the standards for pay and promotion. It is inextricably related to mandatory retirement at age sixty.

In that sense as well, raising the mandatory retirement age is not a matter that can be solved simply by changing the way the personnel system works for employees who have reached the age of sixty. Few companies that have already raised the retirement age have an ability-based grade system; they have a strong tendency to use a specialist system instead. If the raising of the retirement age is to be smoothly implemented, companies essentially will have to change their personnel systems as well. In fact, the main point about raising the retirement age or abolishing mandatory retirement altogether is how easily an individualized supervision system can be put in place. Companies that have raised the retirement age are more likely than those that have not to have clear and standardized evaluation criteria. They have set out rigorous job grade levels and provide their evaluators with adequate training to deal with them.

As long as companies do not have a smoothly functioning, individualized personnel management system, it will be difficult to raise the retirement age or eliminate the mandatory retirement system.

## The mandatory retirement system and hiring

The big question is: does raising the mandatory retirement age lead to a reduction in youth employment? The present state of retirement and recruitment is summarized in table 4-3. A glance at this shows that the percentage of companies which do not hire recent college or high school graduates on an annual basis is higher at firms that have mandatory retirement at age sixty-one or older or that are thinking of introducing such a system than it is at ones with mandatory retirement at age sixty. It may well be that raising the age of retirement does in fact lead to a reduction in the hiring of recent graduates.

On the other hand, however, the opposite may be true: companies may be raising the retirement age in order to maintain a constant level of employment because they are unable to hire sufficient numbers of recent graduates and other young people. In that case, we need to look not at the present situation but at future hiring plans, which serve as a more or less direct indicator of a company's intentions vis-à-vis hiring. Here too, however, the percentage of companies which have no plans to hire new graduates in the future is higher at firms with mandatory retirement at age sixty-one or over. The concern that raising the mandatory retirement age will lead to cutbacks in the hiring of new graduates

**Table 4-3 Hiring Plans and Raising the Mandatory Retirement Age (%)**

| Present state of hiring (%) | | Has a mandatory retirement system for all workers at age 60 | | |
|---|---|---|---|---|
| | | Has no plans to change the present system | | Has decided to change the retirement age to 61 or older or is considering doing so |
| | | | Has a reemploy-ment system | |
| Hiring trends for recent graduates | Does not hire high school graduates annually | 28.7 | 27.1 | 37.8 |
| | Does not hire college graduates annually | 29.7 | 28.2 | 51.8 |
| Future hiring | No plans to hire recent graduates | 34.0 | 31.4 | 25.6 |
| | No plans for mid-career hiring | 37.0 | 36.1 | 1.1 |
| Share of companies (%) | | 80.0 | 43.1 | 1.1 |

*Note*: Recalculation of the 1998 *Survey of Employment Management*

is in fact justified. When it comes to mid-career hiring, there is virtually no difference between companies that have mandatory retirement at age sixty and those that have it at age sixty-one or older. Moreover, the percentage of companies that do not hire recent high school or college graduates annually or do not plan to do so in future is low at firms with a reemployment system (see page 84).

It is also possible that differences in company size or industrial sector may affect the relationship between a rise in the mandatory retirement age and recruitment. In that case, let us consider the effect on hiring plans between those who responded either (1) that they "have a mandatory retirement system for all workers at age sixty-one or older" or (2) that they "have decided to change the retirement age to sixty-one or older or are considering doing so." (For a more detailed look at this question, see "The data speak" at the end of the chapter) The results show that, even discounting differences in company size and industrial sector, the former have a higher probability of not hiring high school or college graduates annually and a lower probability of having any future

| Has a mandatory retirement system for all workers at age 61 or older | Has no mandatory retirement system | Has a mandatory retirement system based on job category |
|---|---|---|
| 45.4 | 58.6 | 32.4 |
| 48.1 | 58.6 | 31.1 |
| 40.4 | 40.7 | 43.2 |
| 36.2 | 30.4 | 21.4 |
| 6.2 | 9.4 | 3.3 |

plans to do so. Though the latter also have a high probability of not hiring recent graduates annually, on the other hand, they are more likely to have plans for mid-career and/or new graduate hiring in the foreseeable future. It is also possible to confirm that companies with a reemployment system, even those with mandatory retirement at age sixty, have less of a tendency to cut back on hiring.

## Classifying companies that have raised their retirement age

The conclusion we can draw from the above discussion is that there are at least two types of companies which have raised their mandatory retirement age to sixty-one or older. These findings are summarized in table 4-4.

The first type can be described as "responding to the demands of an aging society." This group regards making the best use of its aging employees as a serious issue and has raised the retirement age for that reason. Unlike companies which have kept the mandatory retirement age at sixty and are plagued by a lack of clarity and/or standardization in their employee evaluation criteria, this first type has raised the retirement age despite the problems an aging workforce entails and are proceeding with the implementation of an individualized personnel management system for their employees. There is relatively little sense that continuing to employ older workers is burdensome because companies in this group have already fully factored in the cost of doing so and have accu-

## Table 4-4 Classification of Companies That Have Raised Their Mandatory Retirement Age

| | | (At least) two types of continued employed | |
|---|---|---|---|
| | Traditional type | Response to aging society | Employment expansion |
| Present state of retirement system | Retain mandatory retirement at age 60 | Have raised the retirement age to 61 or older while dealing with the problems of personnel evaluation | Have decided to raise the retirement age or are considering doing so because of the rise in the eligibility age for public pensions, societal demands, etc. |
| Reasons for raising the retirement age | Have not (or cannot) raised the retirement age | Cite as their reason "make use of older workers' experience and skills" | Main reasons cited are "the rise in the eligibility age for public pensions" or "demands of society" |
| Special characteristics | Difficulties making use of older workers if the retirement age were raised | Problem is how to make use of an increasing number of older workers | Some companies can afford to make use of older workers |
| (Expected) background | Existing personnel management system (ability-based grade system, etc.) will basically continue | Aging workforce; difficulty in adjusting employment levels | Business performance relatively sound; labour shortage |
| Personnel management | Confronting the difficulties of individualized management. Problems arising particularly from "lack of standardization and vagueness of evaluation criteria" | Focusing energy on individualized management of employees. Establish precise distinctions in evaluation, deal with drop in morale. Put effort into training evaluators; relatively few problems with lack of positions. Coordination between evaluation results and financial resources. Feel that it is difficult to cultivate young and middle-aged talent and expect to make use of older workers well acquainted with the work instead. | Tend to raise the retirement age since, in addition to a lack of positions (can increase the number of positions), it is hard to make assessments given the different nature of the work, or because the evaluators' training is inadequate (or number of evaluators insufficient). When retirement age raised, intend to achieve a balance in evaluation results and financial resources. |
| Hiring plans | More likely to have plans to hire recent graduates than those that have raised their retirement age. Companies that use a reemployment system, in particular, are more likely to have hiring plans. | Most responded that they had "no annual hiring" of or "no future hiring plans" for new graduates. Raising the retirement age causes concerns about a future labour surplus and leads to cutbacks in plans to hire recent graduates. Impact on mid-career hiring uncertain. | Although no annual hiring of recent graduates, many "have hiring plans" for the future, not just of recent graduates but also mid-career hiring. Aiming at expanding employment regardless of age. |

mulated the knowhow to put them to efficient use. They therefore tend to give priority to older workers and to cut back on the hiring of recent graduates. In the future, as individualized personnel management spreads, it is likely that this type of company will increase. If that happens, there is a danger that the recruitment of recent graduates will be even further reduced.

By contrast, a group of companies that can be called the "employment expansion" type are attempting to raise the mandatory retirement age and at the same time are increasing their hiring of recent graduates. This type of company has done comparatively well even during the recession of the late 1990s and, as a result, has been maintaining or even expanding its employment levels. In short, these companies have a healthy demand for labour regardless of age and can afford to raise their mandatory retirement age to accommodate a rise in the eligibility age for public pension benefits and to meet other demands of an aging society. Most companies in this category tend to be small or medium-sized firms and are unlikely to answer yes if asked whether raising the mandatory retirement age has led them to cut back on new hiring. Some of them also try to make use of older workers in order to compensate for a shortage of trained evaluators and for difficulties in evaluating work of different natures. Such companies are likely to increase when the economy eventually improves and the number of vacancies rises or when a decline in the workforce population leads to a pronounced labour shortage. Current conditions are quite different, however.

In short, some companies have been steadily growing even during the recession; they would like to increase their workforce, regardless of age, because of a chronic labour shortage, and raising the mandatory retirement age is one way of doing so. Others have been forced to raise the retirement age because their workforce is aging, but, as we shall see, they cannot dismiss surplus employees. If we consider only the first type of growth companies, there would seem to be no cause for concern about the effect on youth employment opportunities. But, of course, not all companies are like this; if raising the retirement age becomes public policy and all companies are forced to do so, there is no denying that this may cause serious problems for companies with surplus employees.

The extent to which raising the retirement age will reduce new hiring is just beginning to be seriously examined. No definitive scientific study has as yet been made, however, primarily due to insufficient data on which to base a statistical analysis since only a handful of firms have actually raised their retirement age. Under these circumstances it seems rather risky to demand that the retirement age be raised or that mandatory retirement be abolished altogether on such purely idealistic grounds as a sense of justice or a concern for human rights.

## Is it possible to revise the right of dismissal?

There are two sides to the mandatory retirement issue, but on one point both proponents and opponents agree: if raising the retirement age is to be implemented smoothly, the rules for employment adjustment, or, more specifically, the rules for dismissal, will also have to be changed.

In Japan strong constraints are imposed on an employer's right to fire an employee. Even when a business slump leads to surplus employment, dismissal is avoided as much as possible. Instead, employment levels are adjusted by establishing a uniform mandatory retirement system and by cutting back on new hiring. Although time consuming, this is the method that Japanese companies, primarily large ones, have traditionally used to adjust their employment levels. Were companies forced to raise the mandatory retirement age or abolish the system altogether, however, it would deprive them of an important means of employment adjustment through natural attrition. New rules would have to be drawn up to revise the right of dismissal and make it easier than it is at present to lay off workers under certain circumstances. Without such a revision, there is a danger that raising the mandatory retirement age will increasingly reduce employment opportunities.

Revising the right of dismissal is not all that simple, however. The reason is that it has never been clearly spelled out in any specific provision of the legal code but rather is based on principles that have been set forth over time under case law. Just as workers have a legal right to resign, the law also recognizes an employer's right to dismiss. In the case of an employee whose contract does not specify term of employment, dismissal is legally possible if the employer gives at least thirty days' advance notice or in lieu of notice pays compensation equivalent to thirty days' salary. Since the 1970s, however, a series of legal precedents have been established to prevent abuses to the right of dismissal. Mass dismissals in particular are subject to strict conditions: employers must demonstrate that they have surplus personnel; that they have made every effort to avoid dismissals; that there are reasonable grounds for the choice of the workers to be let go; and that the procedures leading up to dismissal are fair. In effect, these conditions have placed virtually insuperable restrictions on firing workers.

If the right of dismissal had been written into law, it could conceivably be amended, and a new law enacted. But since it is the product of case law, a clear-cut legislative approach such as this would be quite difficult. Furthermore, when handing down their decisions, judges take into consideration socially accepted ideas of justice, and unless there were to be a clear change in Japanese public opinion, it would be absolutely impossible for a judge to decide in favor of easing the current restrictions. A national debate is needed to clarify the specific conditions under which dismissal would be acceptable so that companies and employees can redefine their relationship and make a fresh start.

I do not mean to imply that the present system should be changed immediately. The government might, for example, write into law the current consensus established under case law in order to facilitate administrative guidance to prevent unjustified dismissals. The aim of such a move would merely be to prevent unjustified dismissals, however; this is a far cry from enacting a law that would make it easier than it is now for companies to lay off workers. We can probably expect that individual instances of dismissal will in essence continue to be dealt with in much the same way as they always have been, through a flexible, case-by-case approach based on case law.

For these reasons, it is virtually impossible under the present circumstances to ease restrictions on dismissal as a trade-off for raising the mandatory retirement age. It would therefore be dangerous to go ahead and raise the retirement age on the unrealistic assumption that dismissals may one day become easier. Even though extending employment past sixty may protect the jobs of those who are already employed, we must not forget that it is also likely to lead to even more serious cutbacks in new job opportunities, primarily for young people. In order to protect employment opportunities for older workers who really want to work, it would be more desirable to proceed with a flexible, individualized approach through a reemployment system, or other such methods, rather than extend employment indiscriminately for all older workers by raising the mandatory retirement age. A reemployment system allows a person who has reached the mandatory retirement age of sixty but who wishes to keep on working to retire and then to enter into a new contract with his/her former employer on terms that reflects his/her wishes and abilities. Such a system would have less likelihood of reducing new employment opportunities than raising the mandatory retirement age.

In an age when everything from company performance to individual career patterns is diversifying, it makes no sense to treat all workers alike when it comes to dismissal or to raising the retirement age. As far as the employment of older workers is concerned, the only answer is to allow people to find a solution that will be personally acceptable depending on their individual circumstances. There is no magic wand that will solve the problems of an aging society at a single stroke.

## The data speak

### Raising the mandatory retirement age and hiring plans

The findings introduced in chapter 4 are based on the "Research Report on Measures to Promote Continued Employment into the Early Sixties" (interim report published March 2002) prepared by the Association of Employment Development for Senior Citizens, a millennium project commissioned in fiscal year 2001 by the Ministry of Health, Labour and Welfare. The analysis here was made possible by permission from the research group to recalculate the Ministry's *Survey of Employment Management*. This survey, which has been conducted annually since 1969, studies the actual state of labour management at hiring, after hiring, and at retirement. The companies studied are firms with thirty or more regular employees; nearly 580 firms were selected for the year 2000 survey.

Table 4-5 gives the results of an analysis of how differences in personnel management affect the way companies deal with mandatory retirement. To be more specific, the *Survey of Employment Management* for 1999 and 2000 was used to estimate which of the following types of retirement systems a company with a personnel evaluation system was likely to choose:

- a mandatory retirement system that applies to all workers at age sixty and the company has no plans to change;
- mandatory retirement at age sixty but the company has decided to change the retirement age to sixty-one or older or is considering doing so;
- mandatory retirement that applies to all workers at age sixty-one or older;
- no mandatory retirement system.

The method used is called a multinomial logit model. From it we can learn how the choice of a retirement system is affected by such factors as company size, industrial sector, use of a specialist system or an ability-based grade system, as well as problems related to personnel evaluation systems and the way they operate. The more asterisks beside a figure in

## Table 4-5 Determinants of Mandatory Retirement Systems at Companies

| | Reference groups | Mandatory retirement for all workers at age 61 or over | |
|---|---|---|---|
| | Explanatory variables | Coefficient | Asymptotic t-value |
| Number of regular full-time employees <1,000 or more> | 300–999 | –0.5080 | –3.78*** |
| | 100–299 | –0.5214 | –4.28*** |
| | 30–99 | –1.2126 | –9.81*** |
| Type of system | Has an ability-based grade system | –0.7959 | –12.90*** |
| | Has a specialist system | 0.3984 | 6.36*** |
| Problems <no problems> with the personnel evaluation system or with the way it operates | No job grade levels in order to make assessments more lenient | –0.2236 | –3.58*** |
| | Drop in morale because evaluations are too severe | –0.8122 | –3.03*** |
| | Lack of coordination between evaluation results and financial resources | –0.4624 | –5.38*** |
| | Evaluation results not reflected in promotion because of a lack of positions | –0.3188 | –3.44*** |
| | Not useful for developing skills or cultivating personnel | 0.2335 | 3.59*** |
| | Evaluators' training inadequate | –0.3381 | –5.62*** |
| | Evaluation criteria unclear or hard to standardize | –0.5657 | –9.37*** |
| | Difficult to make assessments without being well-versed in the nature of the job | 0.1482 | 2.48** |
| | Difficult to assess persons doing work of different natures | 0.0181 | 0.32 |
| | Other | –0.9312 | –5.07*** |
| | Constant | –2.0445 | –15.20*** |
| | Restored sample number (reference group = 44,401) | 1,478 | |
| | LR $\chi^2$ / 7198.49<br>Pseudo $R^2$ | | |

*Source:* The 1999 and 2000 *Survey of Employment Management* (Ministry of Labour) were used to draw up panel data from which the calculations were made.

*Notes:*

1. The greater the number of asterisks, the higher the statistical reliability of the results. A single asterisk indicates a 10% level of statistical reliability; two asterisks, a 5% level; and three asterisks, a 1% level. Reference groups are given in angle brackets. For example, the findings for company size refer to the probability for each group when compared to companies with 1,000 or more employees.
2. In addition to the explanatory variables given above, an industrial sector dummy is also included to control for industrial differences.

**with Personnel Evaluation Systems**

| Mandatory retirement at age 60 but have decided to raise it to 61 or over or is considering doing so | | No mandatory retirement system | |
|---|---|---|---|
| Coefficient | Asymptotic t-value | Coefficient | Asymptotic t-value |
| –0.4047 | –2.53*** | 1.3611 | 1.85* |
| –0.3294 | –2.31*** | 0.9737 | 1.34 |
| 1.0932 | 8.09*** | 4.0001 | 5.60*** |
| –0.1081 | –2.33*** | –1.3267 | –18.85*** |
| –0.0069 | –0.12 | 0.3810 | 5.15*** |
| 0.0428 | 0.90 | –1.1039 | –13.84*** |
| –32.8796 | 0.00 | –2.0825 | –5.96*** |
| 0.5385 | 9.85*** | 0.9012 | 12.34*** |
| 0.2000 | 3.26*** | 0.9127 | 11.15*** |
| –0.1031 | –1.94 | –0.0378 | –0.48 |
| 0.5719 | 11.99*** | –0.7031 | –10.10*** |
| –0.8246 | –16.50*** | –0.9024 | –13.03*** |
| –0.4688 | –8.54*** | 0.1960 | 3.21*** |
| 0.1921 | 4.22*** | 1.3156 | 20.38*** |
| 0.4546 | 4.45*** | 1.6790 | 17.10*** |
| –3.6647 | –25.03*** | –8.5266 | –11.80*** |
| 2,512 | | 1,714 | |
| 7198.49 | | | |
| 0.1507 | | | |

3. The restored sample number is the number estimated for the whole rather than for the extracted sample. If the mandatory retirement system is not given here, the company "has mandatory retirement at age 60 and no plans to change." When the estimated coefficient is a negative number (e.g., for "Have an ability-based grade system") this means that the probability is high that the company will keep mandatory retirement at age 60.

positive and the t-value has an asterisk/asterisks, companies were more likely to choose the system in question. Conversely, when it is negative with an asterisk/asterisks, they are unlikely to choose that system. If a number, whether positive or negative, has no asterisks, that item has no effect on a firm's choice. For example, the coefficient for small companies with thirty to ninety-nine employees that have a mandatory retirement age of sixty-one or older is minus 1.2126 and the t-value has three asterisks. This means that raising the retirement age is rare for such companies. Conversely, the coefficient for companies with thirty to ninety-nine employees that do not have a mandatory retirement system for all workers is 4.0001 and the t-value has three asterisks. This means that many small companies have never had any mandatory retirement system in the first place.

If the coefficients for all choices are minus, none of the systems is likely to be

If the coefficients for all choices are minus, none of the systems is likely to be chosen. This increases the probability that a company "has a mandatory retirement at age sixty and has no plans to change." For example, the coefficients for the item "has an ability-based grade system" are minus in all cases and the t-values have three asterisks. Hence, we can conclude that companies with an ability-based grade system have a strong tendency to keep mandatory retirement for all workers at age sixty. An "ability-based grade system" refers to an occupational competency system used primarily at big companies. Such companies, regardless of size or industrial sector, are highly likely to have "mandatory retirement for all workers at age sixty and no plans to change." Conversely, in the case of companies with a specialist system, the choices "have mandatory retirement for all workers at age sixty-one or older" or "have no retirement system" have a positive coefficient and three asterisks. In other words, such companies have a strong tendency either to raise the retirement age or not to have a mandatory retirement system at all.

When companies responded that "evaluation criteria are unclear or hard to standardize," a response that serves as a proxy indicator for problems related to personnel evaluations, all items are negative with three asterisks; this means there is a high probability of having a mandatory retirement system and no intention of changing it. Conversely, companies that responded that "evaluation is difficult without being well-versed in the nature of the job" were most likely to have raised the retirement age or not to have a mandatory retirement system for all workers.

From these results it emerges that raising the retirement age is difficult unless a company has clear standards and takes an individualized approach to personnel management based on the type of work or the nature of the job.

Using the *Survey of Employment Management* for 1998, table 4-6 analyzes the factors that affect annual hiring conditions for recent graduates as well as future hiring plans at companies with a mandatory retirement system that is applicable to all workers. The method of analysis used is called the probit model. When the coefficients in the table are plus (minus), it means there is a high probability that these factors facilitate ates annually," the coefficient for companies with thirty to ninety-nine employees is 0.2482; this is higher than for companies of other sizes, and there are three asterisks. This means that small and medium-sized companies with thirty to ninety-nine employees have a higher probability of not hiring any recent high school graduates in an ordinary year. Similarly, at companies which "have mandatory retirement for all workers at age of sixty-one or older" the coefficient for not hiring recent high school and college graduates is 0.1524 and 0.1703, respectively; both are positive numbers and have three asterisks.

These findings are described as having a "limiting effect"; they indicate that the probability of not hiring recent high school or college graduates annually is, on average, fifteen to seventeen percent lower at these companies than at those that have kept mandatory retirement at age sixty. From this it can be determined that raising the age of mandatory retirement reduces a company's plans to hire new graduates. We should point out here, however, that there may conceivably be a reverse cause-and-effect relation, i.e., companies may raise their mandatory retirement age to make up for a shortage of workers because they are unable to hire new graduates. In order to measure the number of vacancies at a company more or less directly, our focus shifts to whether or not a company has any future hiring plans as opposed to whether or not it is actually hiring. The coefficient for the question "Do you have any plans to hire new graduates in the future?" this time is minus 0.1000 at companies that have raised the mandatory retirement age; it is negative and has three asterisks. In short, companies that have raised the retirement age for all workers to sixty-one or older have a lower probability of having future hiring plans.

As we can see from these results, there is an undeniable possibility that raising the retirement age reduces the recruitment of young people, particularly recent graduates. At companies that have a reemployment system as a post-retirement measure, however, the probability is low that they will not hire recent graduates annually and high that they will have future hiring plans. From this we can conclude that there is less of an effect on the hiring of recent graduates at companies that are tackling the retirement issue by dealing individually with those who have

**Table 4-6 Determinants for Plans to Hire New Graduates or for Mid-Career Hiring**
**(Reference sample = companies that "have mandatory retirement for all workers at age 60 and no plans to change")**

| | | Does not hire recent high school graduates annually | |
|---|---|---|---|
| | Explanatory variables | Limiting effect | Asymptotic t-value |
| Number of regular full-time employees <1,000 or more> | 300–999 | 0.0584 | 4.40*** |
| | 100–299 | 0.0935 | 7.68*** |
| | 30–99 | 0.2482 | 23.97*** |
| Retirement system <Mandatory retirement at age 60> | Has mandatory retirement for all workers at age 61 or older | 0.1524 | 25.45*** |
| | Has decided to raise mandatory retirement age to 61 or older or is considering doing so | 0.1003 | 7.34*** |
| Post-retirement measures <None> | Has a continued employment system | 0.0571 | 16.80*** |
| | Has a reemployment system | –0.0283 | –9.36*** |
| | Restored sample number | 95,462 | |
| | LR $\chi^2$ | 9382.70 | |
| | Pseudo $R^2$ | 0.0805 | |

*Source:* Recalculation of the 1998 *Survey of Employment Management*

*Notes:* 1. The greater the number of asterisks, the higher the statistical reliability of the results. A single asterisk indicates a 10% level of statistical reliability; two asterisks, a 5% level; and three asterisks, a 1% level. Reference groups are given in angle brackets. For example, the reference group for "Retirement system" is companies with "Mandatory retirement at age 60."

2. In addition to the explanatory variables given above, an industrial sector dummy is also included to control for industrial differences.

3. "Limiting effect" measures how much the probability of each item varies in contrast to average conditions.

ling the retirement issue by dealing individually with those who have reached retirement age and providing continued employment through a reemployment system.

| All companies with a mandatory retirement system applicable to all workers | | | |
|---|---|---|---|
| Does not hire recent college graduates annually | | Plans to hire new graduates in the future | |
| Limiting effect | Asymptotic t-value | Limiting effect | Asymptotic t-value |
| 0.3855 | 12.06*** | −0.2312 | −14.45*** |
| 0.5401 | 18.30*** | −0.3835 | −26.29*** |
| 0.5340 | 26.36*** | −0.4646 | −36.77*** |
| 0.1703 | 28.35*** | −0.1000 | −14.03*** |
| 0.2572 | 18.12*** | 0.1601 | 10.91*** |
| 0.0526 | 15.40*** | −0.0401 | −9.89*** |
| −0.0497 | −16.18*** | 0.0772 | 21.65*** |
| 95,462 | | 81,586 | |
| 15737.54<br>0.1326 | | 9023.30<br>0.0821 | |

# Chapter 5

# The Income Gap and the Job Gap

## Wage disparity and a mounting sense of inequality

"If one thinks about it, there is a word in Japan that is harmful and stress inducing. That word is *gambare*." This remark was made by Oda Mikio, who won Japan's first Olympic gold medal in the triple jump at the 1928 Amsterdam Olympics. Yet, despite his concerns, to this very day the Japanese word used when urging someone on is still *gambare*, and the word to denote determination is still *gambaru*. The nuances and resonances that these terms have will inevitably sound different in a society in which those who work hard can expect something will come of their efforts as opposed to one in which it doesn't matter how hard one tries. The picture that emerges from *Fubyōdō Shakai Nihon* (Japan, the Inequitable Society) by sociologist Satō Toshiki is that Japan is well on its way to becoming the latter type of society.

The data used in Satō's book is taken from the *Survey of Social Stratification and Mobility* (the SSM survey, for short), which has been conducted every ten years since 1955 and which is an invaluable resource for Japanese sociology. From it, it is possible to observe the relationship between the occupations of survey respondents at age forty and the primary occupations of their fathers. This observation led to the discovery that a father's socio-economic status reproduces itself in the status of his son. Simply put, the likelihood of being employed at age forty in an elite, white collar, professional or managerial position is determined by whether or not one's father had been an upper-level white collar worker.

Intergenerational upward mobility began to reverse itself just around the time of the baby boomers. Before then, there had been a tendency for children to become elite white collar workers even though their parents were not, but this began to weaken when the intracohort selection system reached a saturation point and was unable to cope with the enormous size of the baby boom generation. Their entrance into the job market marks the dividing line; thereafter, in a saturated middle class, the connection between a father's occupational status and that of his son strengthened, and it became easy for persons whose fathers were elite white collar workers to become elite white collar workers themselves. Since the mid-1980s Japan's elite society, which had for the most part been open, has been transformed into one that is closed to all but a few. This means the collapse of any prospect of entering the middle class and the emergence of a new class-based society in which individual effort no longer matters. Japan is on its way to becoming a society in which the elite have lost a sense of *noblesse oblige*, and the rest have no hope and no incentive to work hard.

An intergenerational reproductive mechanism that churns out a second generation of intellectual elites in professional and managerial positions—such a mechanism has an impact not only on the transmission of status and schooling but even on access to new forms of knowledge such as computer literacy. According to the 1995 SSM survey, a father's primary occupation has an effect on whether his son has a personal computer or not. The growing intergenerational effect on the acquisition of both traditional and more recent forms of knowledge has the potential of widening not only present disparities but future ones as well.

*Fubyōdō Shakai Nihon* also sounds an alarm about economic and workplace reforms. Most discussions about reform tend to be predicated first on providing a level playing field and then driving home the *ex post facto* need for personal responsibility. But is this scenario, in fact, correct? The key to reading this book is Professor Satō's statement that "equal opportunity is only recognized in hindsight": one can only say with certainty that the playing field was *not* level when the status someone ultimately achieves is related to past circumstances over which that person has no control—the social and occupational status of his father, for instance. The term "equal opportunity" tends to conjure up an image of competitors in a 100-meter race all lined up at the same starting line. But we know from the real world that the only thing that matters is not the opening sprint or a runner's form during the race but how many seconds it takes to cross the finish line. And we can infer from their finishing times that certain competitors began the race from well back (or in front) of the starting line.

The impossibility of anyone ever being entirely able to grasp the situation in which another person finds him/herself is known in economics as imperfect (or asymmetric) information. If one considers the true nature of society to be asymmetric, then Professor Satō's observation that equal opportunity is only recognized in hindsight is persuasive. All the talk about providing equal opportunity or a level playing field is merely a nice-sounding slogan. And when one realizes that outcomes and achievements cannot be attributed solely to an individual him/herself, then the very definition of personal responsibility loses its meaning. "Achievement" and "ability first" become empty words. People whose goal is to win the race through their ability alone, and yet are unaware that vested rights—such as the family into which they were born—have given them a head start, are not likely to develop a sense of social responsibility. It would be hard to describe the theme of this book as cheerful or optimistic. Nevertheless, *Fubyōdō Shakai Nihon* has been a best-seller. Why was this book, by no means an easy read, so well received? Professor Satō's humor and the insight with which he explains social change are not the only reasons for its popularity with the reading public. We must assume that his book taps into a steadily mounting sense of inequality in the popular consciousness.

If that is the case, then, what is causing this growing perception of inequality? Not all researchers agree that, statistically speaking, income differentials or wage differentials are widening. Does that mean there is a problem with the statistics? According to the *Wage Census*, volume 1, table 3 (Ministry of Health, Labour and Welfare), which is often used to detect trends in wage differentials, the gap is holding steady. This statistical survey, however, targets only regular employees at private sector workplaces with ten or more employees and so accounts for just sixty percent of all male workers and just thirty percent of all female workers.

Is it the media and mass communications, then, that are to blame for having whipped up this mounting sense of inequality? Even the *Wage Census*, which shows no wage gaps across the board, indicates that there is one group for whom wage differentials are widening: male college graduates in their forties. The media make much of the fact that the introduction of performance-based pay will intensify the division between winners and losers. Have middle-aged and older white collar workers, beset by fears that they may be the losers in a performance-based workplace, bought into this propaganda?

## Is the gap widening?

Since the end of the 1990s, there has been an ongoing debate about whether wage differentials in Japan are becoming more inequitable. As I mentioned in the prologue, Tachibanaki Toshiaki, a proponent of the view that the gap is widening, observes in his book *Nihon no Keizai Kakusa* (Japan's Economic Disparities) that Japanese society has been steadily moving toward ever greater inequality. On the other hand, economists Ohtake Fumio, Ōta Kiyoshi, and others maintain that the widening gap is more apparent than real—the result of a demographic increase in the number of elderly among whom wage disparity tends to be large—and that the structure of the differentials is actually quite stable (Ōta Kiyoshi, *Dēta de Yomu Seikatsu no Yutakasa* [Affluence as Read from the Data] [Tokyo: Tōyō Keizai Shimbunsha, 1999]; Ohtake Fumio, "Kyūjū nendai no Shotoku Kakusa" [Wage Differentials in the 1990s],*Nihon Rōdō Kenkyū Zasshi* [Japanese Journal of Labour Studies], July 2000).

A number of reasons can account for the divergence of opinions on both sides: differences in data, in the scope of the survey, in distribution methods, to name but a few. It is not my intention here to judge which side is correct; rather, I would like to focus on trends in wage differentials among young workers which are likely to determine future trends in wage differentials and, in turn, in income differentials as a whole.

Figure 5-1 attempts to show the extent to which wage differentials grew between the early 1980s and the late 1990s within social strata

**Fig. 5-1 Wage Differentials between the Top and Bottom 10th Percentiles** (By age, gender, and level of education)

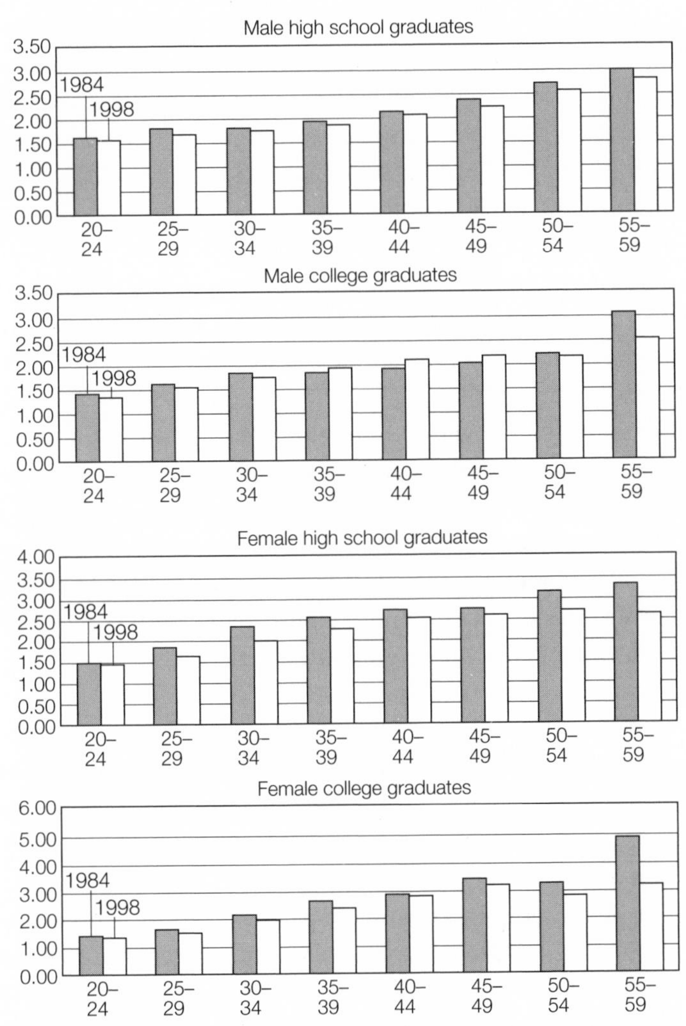


*Source*: Compiled from the Ministry of Health, Labour and Welfare, *Basic Survey on Wage Structure (Wage Census)*

defined by gender, age, and level of education. To measure these differentials I adopted the following method, which is often used to study income distribution. First, rank wage earners in order beginning with those at the lowest end of the scale; then divide each group into 100 equal parts based on the number of people in each group. Finally, calculate how many times higher the salary is for the group in the top tenth percentile of each class as compared to the group in the bottom ninetieth percentile. In the chart for male high school graduates, for example, the height of the bar graph for those between the ages of forty and forty-four was "2" in both 1984 and in 1998. This means that male high school graduates in their early forties who were in the top tenth percentile by income receive a monthly salary approximately twice that of those in the bottom tenth percentile.

The most important message to take from these charts is that for most classes no widening trend can be observed; rather, differentials are narrowing, a phenomenon that deserves to be called a "standardization of wages." This is particularly true for young people regardless of gender or education; wage differentials for them are, in fact, moving in the exact opposite direction from what is generally accepted to be the case.

The only class in which a trend conformable with widening can be found is among male college graduates in their late thirties to forties. Behind this trend is the fact that most male college graduates in this age cohort fall into the category of white collar workers at large companies where performance-based pay systems are gradually being introduced. The fact is, however, that in virtually every other class it is impossible to detect any signs of a performance-based system or a widening in compensation differentials that accompany it.

The popular belief in growing disparities rests on a preoccupation with middle-aged and older male college graduates and does not take into consideration the circumstances in which young people, non-college graduates, and women find themselves. The vast majority of Japanese are far removed from the outcry about performance-based pay or the widening differentials that go along with it. Nevertheless, recent discussions make it seem as though wage distributions are widening for all social strata.

## Performance-based pay and perceptions of disparity

When it comes to disparity and inequality, why is there a gap between perception and reality? The first conceivable reason may be the uneasiness generated by the publicity that surrounds performance-based pay. The media keep emphasizing the impasse that has resulted from a seniority-based wage and benefit system and the need to replace this with one based on individual performance. If, as the term suggests, a performance-based system causes wage disparities to widen between employees who achieve results and those who do not, then, it is only natural that the new personnel system would cause feelings of stress and anxiety for anyone without a lot of self-confidence.

At present, however, most companies are only in the process of introducing a performance-based system or are still at the planning stage. Viewed in this light, it might be more reasonable to assume that as yet there is no clear link between performance-based pay and widening disparities. Moreover, it is a bit too hasty to conclude that any future widening that may result from a performance-based system ought to be a cause for concern for society as a whole. The system under review is aimed primarily at those in management-level positions; thus far, few companies are attempting to introduce it across the board for ordinary employees. Moreover, even where companies have introduced systems of remuneration based on individual ability and performance, there is absolutely no proof whatsoever that pay gaps have actually widened as a result.

> A shift from a labour surplus to a labour shortage, the aging of Japan's employment structure, the rise in employees' educational levels in tandem with a rise in the percentage of those who go on to higher education, and the steep climb in salary levels that this will entail, will lead to the need for elitism and a growing demand to move away from a pay system based primarily on age (and accompanied by demands to raise the retirement age) to one based primarily on ability.

This passage comes from "Nōryokushugi Kanri—Sono Riron to Jissen" (Merit-based Management: Theory and Practice), the report of the Japan Federation of Employers' Associations' study group on merit-based management (for further details see the introduction to Satō Hiroki, *Rīdeingusu: Nihon no Rōdō 5: Koyō Kanri* [Readings: Japanese Labour 5: Employment Management] [Tokyo: The Japan Institute of Labour, 1999). It was published not in the 1990s but in 1969. Future generations looking back over the history of the Japanese labour market will probably be disconcerted to learn that the same debate has occurred over and over again in the latter half of the twentieth century. The uneasiness accompanying performance-based pay may actually be anxiety over the fact that, while the need to link pay to performance is all too well known, nothing at all has changed or is about to change.

There have been loud calls that greater emphasis be given to management skills in determining pay for the managerial class, which is made up of middle-aged or older male college graduates, who tend to be in excess supply thanks to a rapidly aging and better educated workforce. Yet, in the final analysis, the performance-based system that has arrived on the scene with such fanfare is one in name only. Nothing has changed that ought to have changed, including the way management positions are determined, and, as a result, a feeling akin to despair is beginning to cause uneasiness about the future.

To be sure, when we look at the *Wage Census* and other data, it is possible to detect a gradual widening trend in wage differentials for male college graduates in their forties, primarily at large companies with a 1,000 employees or more. As figure 5-1 shows, this trend is found among college graduates in their late thirties and forties, though not in other age groups. There is a tendency to regard this as proof that a performance-based system is having an impact on middle-aged and older college graduates and that a skill-based diversification among workers is gradually beginning to manifest itself in the form of wage differentials. On the other hand, however, it is also possible that, rather than reflecting greater pay inequality *within* companies, this gap shows widening wage disparities *between* companies resulting from divergences in individual corporate performance. Furthermore, while internal advancement and a compensation system based primarily on age, length of service, and so forth remain basically unchanged, another cause for the apparently widening gap may be a gradual polarization in the average number of years of continuous service at the same company. Signs of this can, in fact, be found in figure 5-2. Generally speaking, most Japanese male college graduates in their forties have worked for the same company for around twenty years. But throughout the 1990s the percentage has been dropping for those with between fifteen to nineteen and between twenty and twenty-four years of service. Conversely, there has been a rise in the percentage of those with around ten years of service (those with between five to nine and between ten to fourteen years). This presumably reflects the fact that workers, who were then in their thirties, changed jobs during the economic boom of late 1980s and early 1990s. At the same time, however, the percentage of those who have worked at the same company for twenty-five years or more has slightly increased, a trend that runs counter to the supposed collapse of long-term employment. Thus, a polarizing trend is slowly emerging among middle-aged and older college graduates between those who have long-term employment and those who do not. As a result, they are being divided into two groups: those who have benefited from the old system of internal advancement and seniority-based pay and those who have not. It may be this polarization that is giving rise to the wage gap.

In any event, it cannot necessarily be said that the introduction of a performance-based pay system is the direct cause of widening disparities nationwide.

## The job gap as seen from the perspective of working hours

There is a divergence between perceptions of disparity and the statistical facts. One more reason for this may be that it is not a widening *wage* gap that is now occurring but a widening *job* gap.

Imagine there are two people, A and B. The nature of their jobs and their salary levels are exactly identical, and both of them are satisfied with this situation. But, at some point, while A's job remains the same, B's become incredibly difficult and demanding. Yet, in spite of this, their salary levels remain virtually unchanged. As a result of the huge disparity that has arisen in the nature of their work, B feels dissatisfied about the gap between his job and A's. For statistical purposes, however, the wage gap between A and B is almost exactly the same as it used to be. Might it not be that a situation similar to this is spreading throughout

**Fig. 5-2 Length of Service at the Same Company**
**(Male college graduates aged 40–49)**

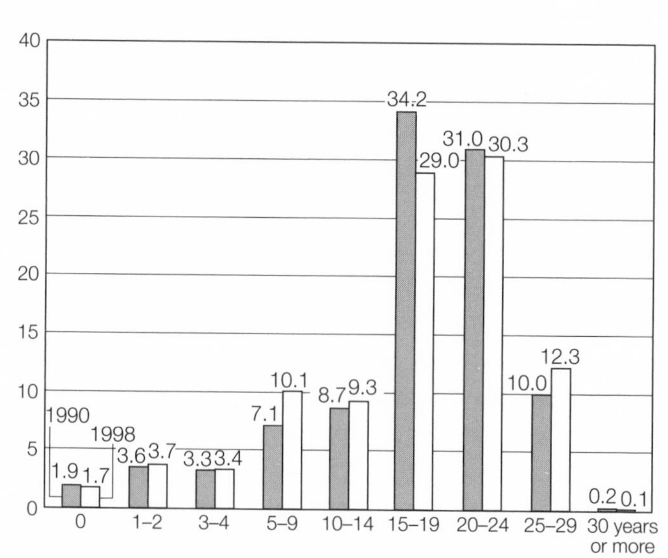


*Source*: Ministry of Health,Labour and Welfare, *Basic Survey on Wage Structure (Wage Census)*

Japan, and that this explains why the statistics show no widening in wage differentials despite a growing nationwide perception of disparity? The fact is that what we might call a "job gap" or a "gap in working conditions" may perhaps be on its way to becoming more serious than the wage gap.

As an example of the widening job gap, allow me to introduce some data that have not attracted much notice: statistics on working hours. From the 1980s to the beginning of the 1990s, the long hours that Japanese worked was considered a problem. Today, however, the subject is virtually ignored. In 1985, companies that had introduced a two-day weekend in some form or other accounted for only 49.1 percent or roughly half of all firms with thirty or more regular employees; by 1997, however, the vast majority, ninety percent, had adopted a two-day weekend (Ministry of Health, Labour and Welfare, *Comprehensive Survey on Wages and Working Hours*).

On the whole, then, working hours are getting shorter, but when we break down this general trend by age groups, what differences do we find? It has recently been said that there is a growing tendency, primarily among young people, to attach more importance to their private lives than to their jobs and to avoid working long hours. Is this true? Figure 5-3 shows the percentage of those working 200 or more days a year who put in long hours—ordinarily sixty or more hours a week. A glance tells us that the percentages dropped significantly every year from the 1980s to the early 1990s, and that this downward trend has basically continued throughout the 1990s. When we look at these percentages by age groups, however, clear differences can be found in the degree of the decline. Among men age forty-five to forty-nine, for example, those working long hours dropped nearly two percent, from 14.7 percent in 1992 to 12.8 percent in 1997; on the other hand, there was hardly any change during this period among men in the thirty- to- thirty-four age group. For women as well, despite a decline among those in relatively high age groups, the percentages for women in their twenties were virtually unchanged. A decline in the percentages of those working long hours can be found primarily among the middle-aged and older; among younger cohorts it is not all that evident.

Figure 5-4 is even more shocking. It calculates the same percentages but this time not for those who work 200 or more days a year as in figure 5-3, but for those who work 250 days or more. Although the former category comprises people who work mostly at companies that have introduced a two-day weekend, virtually all those in the latter category work at firms with a one-day or a one-and-a-half-day weekend. A closer look shows that, by 1997, the percentage of employees working long hours, which had dropped between 1987 and 1992, was once again climbing back to its earlier levels among males in their thirties and females in their twenties.

Let us look a little further into the actual state of long working hours. Figure 5-5 attempts to show changes in the percentages of those with a thirty-five-hour or more work week who, in fact, put in sixty hours or more a week. After the Plaza Accord in September 1985, the yen rose, and, on a dollar basis, Japan became one of the richest countries in the world in terms of income. Even with those high salary levels, however, it

**Fig. 5-3 Percentage of Those Working More Than 200 Days a Year Who Ordinarily Work More Than 60 Hours a Week**

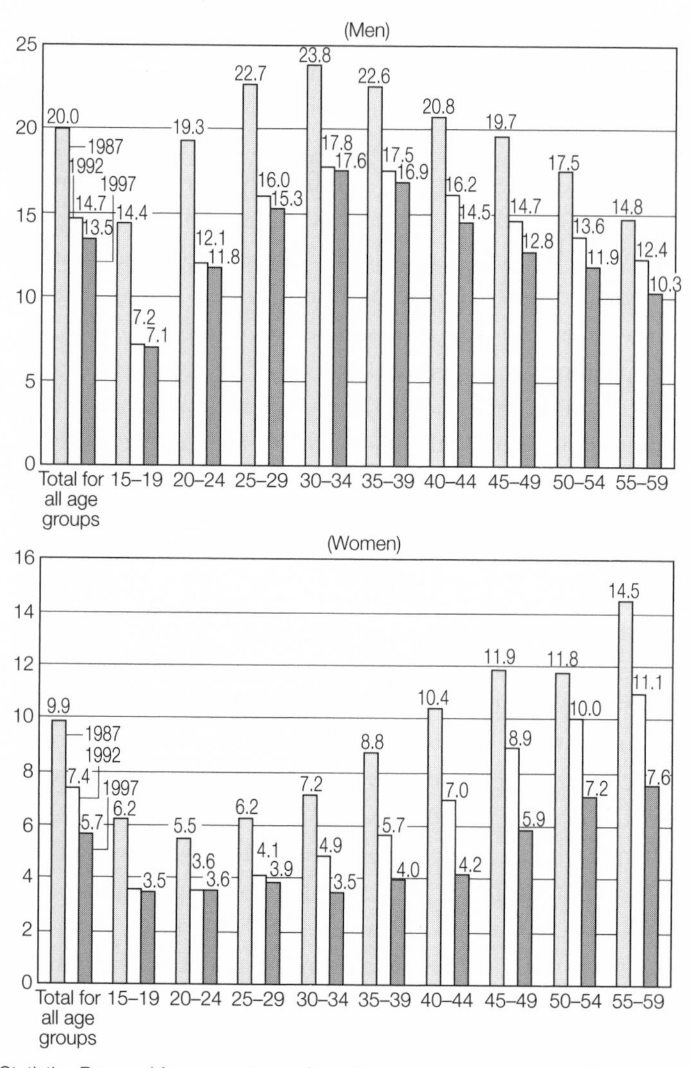


*Source*: Statistics Bureau, Management and Coordination Agency, *Employment Status Survey*

**Fig. 5-4 Percentage of Those Working More Than 250 Days a Year Who Ordinarily Work More Than 60 Hours a Week**

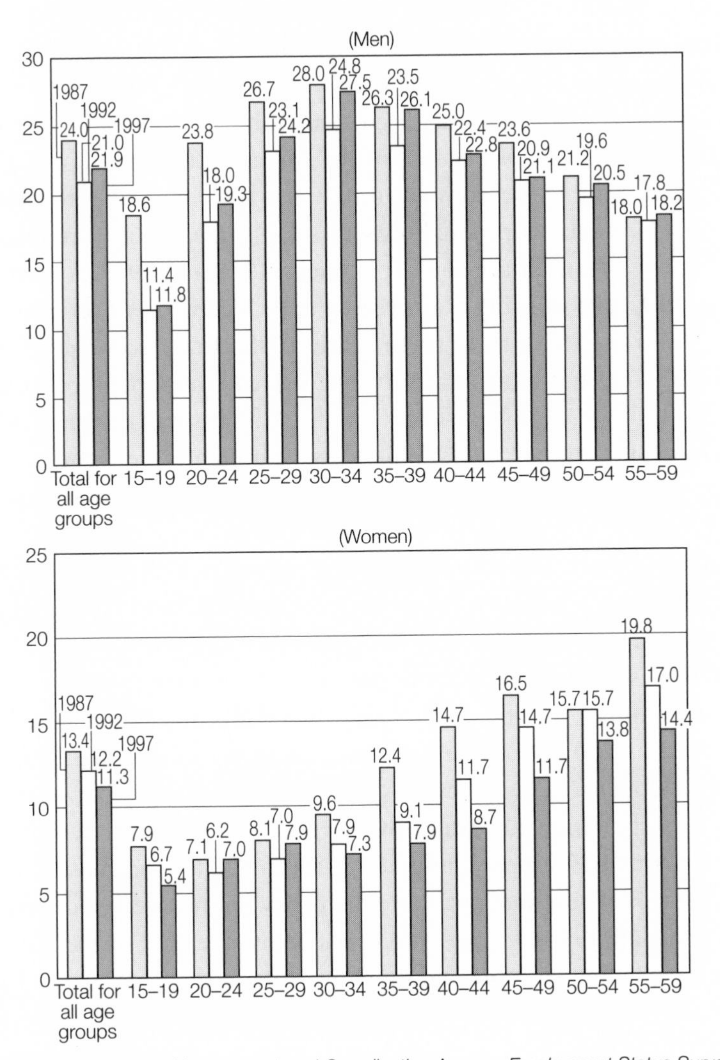


*Source*: Statistics Bureau, Management and Coordination Agency, *Employment Status Survey*

was impossible for Japanese to have any true feeling of affluence, and "Are the Japanese really rich?" became a frequently asked question. Long working hours were often cited as emblematic of Japanese society's lack of true prosperity. Certainly, a glance at this graph shows a rising trend throughout the 1980s among those working more than sixty hours a week at large, small, and mid-sized companies alike.

Thereafter, perhaps because of the spread of the two-day weekend and an increase in the number of national holidays, the percentage of those working sixty or more hours a week dropped sharply as the economy moved from boom to bust between 1989 and 1993. Around the same time, long working hours ceased to be regarded as a serious problem. From the 1980s through the early 1990s, the percentage of those working long hours at relatively large-sized companies with 500 or more employees was significantly lower than at small companies with five to twenty-nine workers. When large companies were compared to small and medium-sized ones, the disparity in working conditions was hard to deny: not only were wages and benefits better, work hours were relatively shorter. This contractionary trend began to reverse itself, however, and, since 1999, there has been a steep rise in the percentage of those at large companies who work sixty or more hours a week. In the year 2000, for example, the number of workers at companies with 500 or more employees who put in fewer than thirty-five hours a week had declined by 250,000, while those who were working more than sixty hours a week had gone up by 180,000. As a result, the gap between companies with 500 or more employees and those with between five and twenty-nine has almost completely disappeared, at least as far as the percentage of those working more than sixty hours a week is concerned. Since the late 1990s, young employees below the level of section chief have been taking on more and more overtime, a situation that is probably becoming the norm in most workplaces at large companies. Some of these young people are working such long hours they are beginning to wonder why they made an effort to go to college and get a job at a famous company since their relatively high salary is not commensurate with the amount of work expected of them.

What does the increase in the number of young people working long hours mean? During the recession, work quotas rose, and since there was

**Fig. 5-5 Employees Working More Than 60 Hours a Week as a Percentage of All Those Who Work More Than 35 Hours a Week by Company Size**
**(Excluding those in the public sector)**

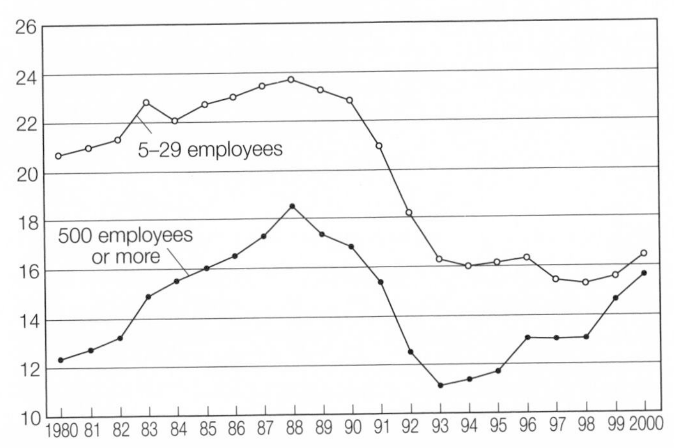


*Source*: Statistics Bureau, Management and Coordination Agency, *Annual Report on the Labour Force Survey*

a freeze on hiring, workloads increased even further. Much attention has been focussed on the rise in the number of young people known as freeters who do not become regular employees but take part-time jobs or temporary employment. Not all young people work only a few hours each week, however; many work long hours, but hardly anyone pays any attention to them. When the youth labour problem is thought of in terms of a widening job gap or a widening gap in working conditions, quite a different image emerges from the stereotypical view of feckless youth conjured up by the complaints about how disgraceful it is that young people are becoming freeters.

## Job change, part-time work, and a dual labour market

When it comes to job change as well, the emphasis has been on changes in young people's attitudes toward work. Young people, it is said, quit their jobs as soon as something unpleasant happens, and no long feel any commitment to work. But that is by no means the whole story. If you listen carefully to young people who have left their jobs and gone to work elsewhere, you are more likely to hear them say, "I could no longer figure out what I was working for," or "I felt that job was stunting my growth as a human being," or "I couldn't stand the thought of how my personality would deteriorate if I kept on working like that." It is not a matter of a decline in young people's work ethic; the fact is that the opportunity to find a job which instills feelings of commitment, of pride in oneself, as well as a sense of personal growth and hope for the future, is limited to all but a handful, and the situation is only getting worse. Isn't this the real reason most young people quit their jobs?

The job gap is not just a problem for young people. It also exists between part-time and full-time employees. Although wage differentials among full-time employees are not widening, the pay gap between full-timers and part-timers is growing. When gaps of this kind exist, most part-timers find them hard to accept. But a closer look at the reasons for their discontent shows that most of them are not necessarily dissatisfied that their pay is too low. Rather, they do not accept being paid low wages and considered part-timers despite the fact that their level of responsibility and degree of freedom is the same as (or, in some cases, even greater than) that of full-time employees. (For further details, see Ministry of Labour, "Pāto Taimu Rōdō ni Kakaru Koyō Kanri Kenkyūkai Hōkoku" [Report of the Employment Management Study Group on Part-time Work]. A summary can be found on pages 115 through 117 of the 2000 edition of the White Paper on Labour.) Regardless of whether one works full time or part time, work that is unfairly apportioned or for which the parameters of responsibility and autonomy are not made clear is apt to cause dissatisfaction, stress, and even despair.

All work is honorable, but there are two types of jobs that are clearly different. The first provides workers with a wealth of on-the-job training and learning opportunities and allows them to improve their incomes and upgrade their skills while they work. The other type offers no skills improvement and no meaningful work because the opportunity to learn anything on the job is so limited. When most people, through no fault of their own, are forced to accept the latter type of work while the former goes only to a select few, it creates what is known as a "dual labour market." In economics, the term "internal labour market" traditionally refers to a workplace environment that provides the former type of job; an environment that provides only the latter is called an "external labour market."

A dual structure is undoubtedly the cause of wage gaps. But what gives rise to a dual labour market in the first place is the job gap—the fact that workers are being divided into two distinct groups: those who find jobs that offer rich opportunities for training and learning and those who do not. Economist Ishikawa Tsuneo, who devoted himself to elucidating distribution problems, warned that a dual structure of this sort has been steadily widening in the Japanese labour market since the 1980s (Ishikawa Tsuneo, *Bumpai no Keizaigaku* [The Economics of Distribution] [Tokyo: University of Tokyo press, 1999], part III, section 4 "Rōdō Shijō no Nijū Kōzō" [The Dual Structure of the Labour Market]). The labour market problem that so concerned Professor Ishikawa is assuming an ever more solid shape. An internal labour market has become remote for most people; they find themselves in an external labour market with fewer and fewer chances to achieve personal growth through their jobs. This is yet another factor behind the nagging sense of job insecurity.

# Chapter 6

# Performance-based Pay and a Sense of Purpose in One's Work

## How are ability and work talked about?

The nagging sense of job insecurity is not simply a matter of having a job or not. To a far greater degree than ever before, drastic changes in the environment—demographic aging, a better-educated workforce, deregulation, computerization, and globalization—are forcing us to confront head on the issue of differences in individual ability. Behind the uneasiness lies the stressful realization that, from now on, everyone without exception will have to face up to having his/her skills assessed.

That does not mean, of course, that Japanese corporate society has previously ignored this issue. In particular, most workers on shop floors at manufacturing companies have been exposed to a far more rigorous evaluation of their skills than their counterparts in other developed countries. Such assessments, however, have centered on a tacit understanding of the latent talent an individual may possess, whereas the current trend attempts to make an open evaluation of tangible differences in individual abilities. One can readily imagine that this is the direction in which the performance-based personnel system now being applied to middle-aged and older white collar workers is heading.

Companies attempting to introduce a performance-based system invariably allude to the "difficulties of the evaluation process." But when we stop to think about it, such difficulties are inevitable. If a total grasp of another person's abilities were possible, the good society would be ruled and regulated by a philosopher king. History teaches us, however, that, despite the problems it entails, the mechanism that sustains a market economy and regulates public interests is basically the impersonal concept of price. No matter how hard one tries, there are limits to what one person can know about another. This fact itself inculcates a spirit of mutual respect and gives rise to societal manners and morals. Yet despite the premise that our understanding of others is essentially imperfect, in the days ahead many will be faced with the contradiction of having to make an open assessment of some other person's skills. If that is so, then, what society really needs is to figure out how to discuss differences in individual abilities and how each of us can cultivate the sensibility and vocabulary for doing so. The important thing will be the slow but honorable task of teaching people while they are still young that differences in a person's job skills have absolutely nothing to do with his/her value as a human being and then to reaffirm this basic point over and over again.

As the baby boom generation approaches the retirement age, ensuring job opportunities for older workers will become more important than ever before. There is also a growing consensus that Japan will have to take a second look at age-related discrimination in employment opportunities. What will be needed then will be individual abilities in the true sense—irrespective of age, gender, or level of education—and a way of evaluating them. The time is approaching when society as a whole will need to discuss seriously what "ability" is and how to deal with differences.

The terms "performance-based" and "merit-based" are often used interchangeably, but they are not the same thing. Japanese personnel management has traditionally espoused a merit-based system. As I noted earlier, the consensus among researchers is that a merit-based evaluation system has already been achieved among plant workers. In that sense, it might be best to understand the performance-based system that companies are now struggling to implement as an attempt to fashion a new kind of merit-based system with the white collar worker in mind. How does the old merit-based system differ from the new performance-based system? Broadly speaking, it involves a shift from paying a salary *to a person* to paying a salary *for a job*. Whether companies can make a smooth transition to a performance-based system will depend on whether or not job descriptions can be made more precise. Without clear and accurate job descriptions, a performance-based system will fail.

Clarifying job descriptions, however, is not simply a matter of determining that a job is in a certain line of business or that it involves making X percent of Y sales in location Z. Not only will setting goals and outcomes be important, even more so will be to clarify how much and what kind of freedom and responsibility an employee must have to get the job done.[1]

## Conditions for implementing a performance-based system

Two opinions coexist about the introduction of a performance-based system. The first is that rapid systemic reforms are needed in order to deal with rapid structural changes in the economy; the second is that overhasty changes will damage labour-management relations and the skill development systems that companies have cultivated over time. From the workers' perspective, assessments differ about how a performance-based system is likely to affect their earnings.

Such concerns are only natural, but people do not work for a salary or for status alone. For many, an even more important consideration is whether the new system makes them feel that what they do is worthwhile and increases their incentive to work. For a performance-based system to make good its goal of raising productivity, worker motivation will have to rise. Will the introduction of a performance-based system actually accomplish this end?

Allow me to introduce the results of a survey on changes in work incentive among white collar workers at large companies where a performance-based system has been introduced. I will defer a more detailed discussion to "The data speak" at the end of this chapter, but, to sum up,

---

1. If we think carefully about it, the concept of *sekinin*—translated here as "responsibility"—is surprisingly unclear in Japanese society. In English "responsibility" or "accountability" can be used depending on the circumstances. By contrast, Japanese society has no strict definition of *sekinin* and no clear awareness of the diversity it may entail. The same applies to the term *jiyū* (freedom).

**Table 6-1 The Relation between the Introduction of a Performance-Based Pay System and the Probability That Work Incentives Will Go Up**

| | Functional conditions of the job | |
|---|---|---|
| | Have been reviewed | Have not been reviewed |
| All workplaces surveyed | 0.37 | 0.21 |
| Those where a performance-based system has been introduced | 0.27 | 0.13 |

*Source*: Genda Yūji, Kambayashi Ryō, and Shinozaki Takehisa, "Shokuba Kankyō no Henka to Hataraku Iyoku, Funiki no Henka" (Changes in the Workplace Environment and Changes in the Atmosphere and the Incentive to Work), *Shokuba to Kigyō no Rōshi Kankei no Saikōchiku* (Rebuilding Labour-Management Relations in the Workplace and the Company) (Japan Productivity Center for Socio-Economic Development, June 1999)

*Note*: Figures indicate the probability that the incentive to work will go up under each circumstance.

the incentive to work was higher at workplaces where, concurrently with the introduction of the new system, clear changes were made to the way work was being done. Table 6-1 gives the estimated results of the probability that introducing a performance-based pay system and improving the functional conditions of a job will lead to a rise in the incentive to work. By "improving the functional conditions of a job," I mean whether a review has been explicitly carried out in the past three years to determine whether the employees' workload, working hours, and responsibilities have increased or decreased; whether their job description, the scope of their discretionary powers, and their work assignments have been clarified; and whether they have been given the opportunity to develop their skills.

A glance at this table shows that the probability of an increase in work incentive was lowest—0.13—at workplaces in which only a performance-based system was introduced while working conditions otherwise remained unchanged. Conversely, among all workplaces surveyed, it was highest—0.37—at those in which a review of functional conditions had been carried out. Even at workplaces in which such a review had been conducted, however, the probability of a rise in incentive was only 0.27 at workplaces where a performance-based system had been introduced. From this we know that the increase is highest at workplaces where functional conditions have improved even though a performance-based system has not been formally introduced. To put it another way, these results signify that the incentive to work will not improve if provisions are made only for the outer trappings of a performance-based system without actually changing the contents of the job itself.

In order for a performance-based system to raise productivity and for the results to be satisfactory, companies will have to come to grips with the issue of clarifying their job descriptions. If they simply go ahead and introduce the new system while allowing job descriptions to remain unclear, it is conceivable that the job gap we saw in the previous chapter will widen even further and that the incentive to work may actually decrease.

## A "training-type" performance-based system

Along with clarifying the job description, there is another key to the success or failure of a performance-based system: skill development. Since, as the term implies, such a system expects results, firms cannot afford to wait around forever to achieve them. Some things may take more time than others, but, be that as it may, in the short or medium term at the very latest, individual employees will be expected to show results. A performance-based system inevitably attaches great importance to an accurate evaluation of tangible results. Although at first glance this may seem contradictory, the success of such a system depends on whether or not it is possible to take a long-term view and ensure that employees have the opportunity to develop their skills. Achieving a balance between short-term-oriented performance evaluations and long-term skill development will require wisdom and resourcefulness.

Figure 6-1 focuses on the atmosphere at workplaces that have introduced a performance-based pay system—to be more precise, the sense that an effort is being made to make the best use of each person's abilities—and how this atmosphere differs at workplaces in which opportunities for employees to develop skills have increased when compared to those in which such opportunities have remained the same or decreased. At workplaces with increased opportunities for skill development, eighteen and forty-eight percent, respectively, of the respondents answered

**Fig. 6-1 The Relation between Opportunities for Skill Development and a Sense That an Effort Is Being Made to Make the Best Use of Each Employee**

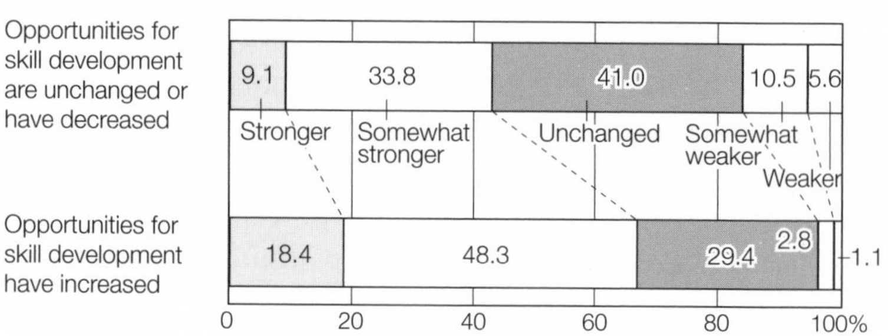


*Source:* Genda Yūji, Kambayashi Ryō, and Shinozaki Takehisa, "Seikashugi to Nōryoku Kaihatsu—Kekka toshite no Rōdō Iyoku" (Performance-based Systems + Skill Development = The Incentive to Work), *Soshiki Kagaku* (Organizational Science) 34, no. 3 (2001)

*Note:* The above results were calculated for workplaces in which a performance-based system had been introduced.

that such an atmosphere had become "stronger" or "somewhat stronger." By contrast, only nine and thirty-four percent, respectively, noted any improvement at workplaces where no increase in skill development opportunities was perceived. Only when a firm makes a concerted effort to expand opportunities for employees to develop their skills concurrently with the introduction of a performance-based pay system will the latter lead to an improvement in the atmosphere of the workplace and a rise in productivity.

In the final analysis, I believe it is meaningless to debate which is more desirable: the existing merit-based system linked to seniority or the new performance-based system toward which we are now striving. If we acknowledge that the economic environment has greatly changed, there can be no alternative but to implement a performance-based system in some form or other. Although there is a tendency to use the term sweepingly, a performance-based system has numerous variations. The foundation upon which performance rests is the skills of each and every employee, and results will differ depending on a company's attitude about how to cultivate and develop those skills. Results achieved by a "laissez-faire-type" system, for example, in which a company adopts an extreme hands off policy toward skill development will be quite different from those achieved by a "training-type" system in which a company tackles this issue even more aggressively than it had previously done.

A training-type performance-based system is one where a company actively promotes skill development on the assumption that employees will apply themselves and where the company does so without considering the costs but while taking into account the risks involved. There are both advantages and disadvantages to such a system. One disadvantage is an increased risk that, once the results are clearly visible, personnel whom the company has gone to great lengths to train will be hired away by another company. And when no results are evident, the company can always make the excuse that training was inadequate. (Complaints about inadequate training aren't valid if a company has made no effort to do anything about it in the first place.) Considering the nature of training, it is hard to expect results over too short a term; to a certain extent, results will have to be evaluated from a long-term perspective.

The advantages outweigh these disadvantages, however. As figure 6-1 shows, expanding the opportunities for employees to develop their skills is indispensable if a performance-based system is to increase their work incentive and improve the workplace atmosphere. In addition, a company that takes an active part in training its employees will be able to create a valuable pool of talent far better attuned to all its own special needs than outsourcing could ever be. When a company provides a practical model of the type of personnel it is looking for, the workforce that results will share its proprietary information and corporate philosophy.

Judging from the results of the figure and table and totaling up the advantages and disadvantages, I believe that, when all is said and done, a training-type performance-based system is the more successful model. "My company rigorously demands results from each and every employee. But, at the same time, it does not stint in providing every possible assistance to those who make an effort to develop their skills." If a company can live up to this statement, it will increase its employees' incentive to work and improve the atmosphere in the workplace.

The difficulty of making job performance evaluations and their vagueness once made are invariably cited as problems in introducing a performance-based system. No matter how detailed and precise the evaluation categories devised to overcome this problem may be, in the final analysis, some vagueness will always remain: no one can completely grasp the abilities of another person. That being the case, the major consideration will be to create an atmosphere in which employees who are dissatisfied by the vagueness of their evaluations feel challenged to do better next time. Providing an abundance of opportunities for skill development means creating opportunities for people such as these to grow and catch up in the future. Conversely, a performance-based system will not be long lived, no matter how many results it may achieve, if it makes employees feel they are being used up or overworked and does not instill any sense of personal growth.

## A performance-based system and hope for the future

In a workplace that is increasingly emphasizing achievement and outcomes, whether or not the boss takes an interest in improving the skills of younger employees will be critical for improving the atmosphere. Whereas the seniority system evolved out of a long-term merit system based on latent skills, a performance-based system is a short-term merit system based on tangible skills. Whether a system is performance-based or not, the boss is always expected to make job assignments that are appropriate. In addition, precisely because a performance-based system is short-term oriented, employees expect a long-term perspective from their boss. In a performance-based workplace, a boss who takes a long-term view and works hard to train and develop the skills of and train his/her staff will win their hearts. Thus, in addition to making appropriate job assignments, an astute boss will try to see to it that each person working under him/her has a long-term perspective. When a boss fulfills this function, he/she will be helping to reinforce a workplace atmosphere of bringing out the best in every worker throughout the workplace. The more weight a workplace gives to the evaluation of achievement and outcomes, the clearer the need for this will become.

Even in a performance-based system that demands short-term results—or, rather, for that very reason—employees expect opportunities to develop their skills within a long-term time frame. What does this mean? In her book *Ikigai ni Tsuite* (A Purpose in Life), psychiatrist Kamiya Mieko explains that a sense of purpose is made up of a number of desires. At a minimum, these include a desire to live, a desire for a sense of fulfillment, a desire for change, a desire for hope for the future, a desire to make a difference, a desire for freedom, a desire for self-actualization, and a desire for meaning and value. Desires such as these that relate to a sense of purpose in one's personal life correspond to those that also give rise to a sense of purpose in one's professional or working life. The evaluation of one's work on the basis of tangible results can satisfy one's desire to make a difference as well as the desire for fulfillment, for self-actualization, and for meaning and value; in that sense, a performance-based system holds out the possibility of leading to a heightened sense of purpose in one's work. The desire for hope for the future is a problem, however. It can be blighted by the demand for short-term results, by blindly pursuing present ends and losing sight of the future. A performance-based system may even prevent some people from feeling any sense of purpose in their work. That sense derives from the expectation that, no matter how hard a job might be right now, some day it will all be worth it.

## Changes that can be implemented right away

In the preceding chapter I said that it is not a widening wage gap that lies behind the pervasive sense of job insecurity, but rather a widening job gap. As long as differences in job descriptions remain unclarified, the gap between people who have an enormous workload and those who do not will continue to grow. A performance-based system per se does not imply that work will be allocated in a clear and open way or that it will lead to the development of a universally acceptable system for making compensation conform to skills. And so, as long as an employee's level of responsibility and degree of autonomy remain vague, introducing the new system will not succeed. Those who quit their jobs because their workload has increased, part-timers who are dissatisfied because their salaries are low, neither of these groups will find any satisfactory reason for working so hard. The same factors also undermine white collar workers' incentive to work.

When considered in this light, the important points are that jobs are always assigned to each and every person in a clear way, that they are assigned in a way acceptable to everyone, that a worker who does not have the skills required for a job he/she would like to do is given the opportunity to develop them. But is there anything that each of us as individuals can do to eliminate the job gap and feel a sense of purpose in our work? It is not easy to try to do something new to reach a new goal. But making a concerted effort *not* to do certain things is achievable. Doing something is very hard, but not doing certain things can be implemented right away.

What should we stop doing? A hint can be found in the words we use. How about not saying, "Try hard!" or "I will try hard"—the words *gambare* and *gambaru* cited at the beginning of the last chapter? Never unthinkingly tell a subordinate, a younger employee, or a friend to "try hard" Make a conscious effort not to use that expression when there is no clear goal in sight. If you have to say something, point your employee in a specific direction by telling him/her what goals you want accomplished and what methods to use in doing so. An employee, too, must never unthinkingly say, "I will try hard." He/she must learn to speak of the goal being aimed at in concrete terms. We all need to put a stop to the use of this vague expression. Clarifying the work relationship between the boss and those who work under him/her is a first step. The Japanese language has too few words other than *gambare* to encourage people and urge them on.

How about making an effort to stop using the expression "I'm busy"? That phrase should not become an excuse for avoiding or refusing to do a job. When you feel yourself about to say, "I'm busy," try to rethink what the work entails and why you are so pressed for time. Really busy people are wary about using the phrase, "I'm busy." A boss should refrain from judging whether an employee seems busy or not. He/she should watch to see whether a busy-seeming employee may be missing out on something because they have too much work. A boss who doesn't do so cannot protect his/her staff members.

Do not say of the way someone is doing a job that "we usually or ordinarily do it this way." There is no such thing as an ordinary job. Something unexpected or problematic always seems to crop up even in jobs that seem simple. The instant someone says the word "usually," he/she has abandoned the effort to try to understand in detail what the job entails.

Try focusing on the job. To that end, avoid vague expressions as much as possible and try speaking about your work in your own words. It is precisely small efforts such as these that will remove the nagging sense of job insecurity. Doesn't the first step on a journey that may seem long but is really short begin with actions such as these?

## The day "*batteki*" loses its meaning

The word *batteki* is made up of two ideograms, the second of which, if we trace its etymology, signifies the act of singling out from among many the one bird with the most gorgeous wings of all. If we check the dictionary for an English equivalent, the translation given is "selection" or "choice," which seems a bit flat. The Japanese word *batteki* has a deeper connotation, one that goes well beyond the mere act of selection or choice. A person of talent, who excels others in ambition and ability, is singled out from obscurity for promotion to a high position and, in turn, becomes a strong motivating factor for change — these expectations are inplicif in *batteki*, and it is precisely in a stagnant society and economy that such hopes grow increasingly higher.

The focus in recent years on this kind of personnel management is, of course, profoundly related to a performance-based system. In such a system, when it comes to employing the best person for a particular job, once the responsibilities and the scope for independent action that go with it have been clarified, criteria such as age and level of schooling no longer have any meaning. The only thing that matters is that the person chosen can do this particular job with this particular degree of freedom. When that happens, *batteki* will lose the connotation of being a "once in a blue moon" event and become a natural occurrence.

All things considered, the ultimate end of a performance-based system will be reached when it becomes the norm for an able person who has achieved results to be given an important position without any regard whatsoever to the year he/she entered the company or where he/she went to school. Promotion in lockstep with others who joined the company at the same time will become the exception not the rule. When that happens, the word *batteki,* which implies that a person with only a few years of service can leapfrog over more senior colleagues into an executive position, will become unnecessary; it will have outlived its usefulness.

What kind of person does the word *batteki* describe? Do many people wish to be singled out for promotion in this way?

Every other year since 1986, a survey has been conducted to explore changes in people's actions and attitudes (the Hakuhodo Institute of Life and Living's Set Point survey of men and women between the ages of twenty and sixty-nine, living in the Tokyo, Osaka, and Kobe areas). It asks detailed questions about the respondents' thoughts on food, clothing, and shelter, as well as topics such as love, family, and work. On the topic of work, the percentage who responded that they preferred to be in an easy, undemanding position went from seventy-three percent in 1990 up to seventy-eight percent in 2000. As far as we can judge from these results, it would not appear that many people want to be singled out for advancement or to hold a high position.

In fact, there are hardly any surveys on what sort of people are singled out for promotion, and no one knows for certain what characteristics they may have in common. Deep down, however, I believe there are one or two prerequisites that such people must have. I once had the opportunity to talk with a former head of the Matsushita Institute of Government and Management. The Institute, he told me, gives great weight to the interview when selecting prospective students, and it has been a tradition since the days of Matsushita Kōnosuke, the founder of Matsushita Electrical Industrial Co., Ltd., to regard just two things as particularly important: whether the candidate being interviewed has charisma and appears to be lucky. I have heard many descriptions of what it takes to be a venture capitalist or an entrepreneur, but I have never come across anything that seemed to sum up the necessary qualities for an independent person as well as these two terms.

What does it mean to appear to be lucky? Make no mistake, I don't think it matters whether or not such a person is actually lucky; the important thing is to *appear* to be lucky. I have no idea whether graduates of the Matsushita Institute are lucky or not. In a crisis, however, an outstanding politician or an outstanding manager is well aware that, even if one puts in the maximum effort, it is impossible do everything by one's self. Such people must therefore be flexible enough to listen humbly to the voices of those around them and enlist their aid to weather the storm. Such a person somehow or other appears to be lucky and has charisma. From an employment perspective, they have a supple grasp of what makes other people tick and the ability inspire them.

When I related this conversation to others, some of them understood immediately what the two terms signified whereas others were mystified by them. It will be increasingly important, I believe, to define precisely what it means to have these two qualities. In any event, a person employed in a responsible position will always be expected to make high-level decisions and will constantly come up against difficult situations that far exceed his/her own abilities. In situations like these, which demand that tough choices be made, such people will rely on a circle of dependable supporters or, to put it another way, a network of outstanding talent. People who appear to be lucky and have charisma have just such a network to draw on. These two qualities are necessary, I believe, even for people who have been singled out for success.

*Batteki* has an even greater significance in the training-type performance-based system that we looked at earlier. It is not simply a matter of a person being chosen because he/she consistently produces results. Rather, the singling out process can be used to challenge someone who had previously suffered a setback and give him/her a second chance. Giving someone who has thus far gone unrewarded a chance to show off his/her ability is precisely what makes this sort of story dramatic. The unexpectedness of the choice causes surprise in a good sense and motivates and inspires fellow workers.

In addition to arousing expectations, *batteki* must include the element of surprise and convey the sense that something interesting is about to happen. It is by no means the case, however, that a personnel system based on singling out the right person for promotion will by definition be regarded by everyone in a favorable light. Those who are passed over are unlikely to find the process particularly pleasant. The person selected in this way must accept as only natural being the object of malicious gossip, having his/her abilities doubted, and the personnel system criticized as unfair. It is precisely such hardships that make being singled out for promotion such a special and rare event. They are also the reason that most people would prefer not to be employed in such a position and would rather have an undemanding job.

Far more than any other talent they may have, the ability to endure adversity gives those singled out for promotion an indescribable aura of appearing to be lucky and having charisma. If good luck and charisma are thought to be natural endowments, only those who have these special gifts ought to be singled out for promotion. The successful person will have enemies, but he/she will have far more allies. He/she will be supported by a strong personal network that will help beat back adversity. Not only will such a person have the strong backing of supporters, he/she will be able to inspire expectations in the younger generation and make them feel that something is about to happen. This will be a deciding factor in his/her success.

A performance-based system in the true sense—i.e., an environment that can cultivate people who have ability but also have luck and charisma—will make the best use of workers and make them feel a sense of purpose in their work; such an environment is precisely what will make the *batteki* singling-out process obsolete.

The data speak

## Performance-based pay and the incentive to work

In order to increase the incentive to work among white collar workers it is necessary to change the pay system and improve the functional conditions of their jobs, e.g., clarify their job assignment and provide opportunities to upgrade their skills. Here I will examine in detail how improving functional conditions improves the incentive to work.

In what follows, I use a questionnaire on work and life in the workplace carried out among white collar workers (except those in management positions) at twenty-seven large companies in September 1998 by the Japan Productivity Center for Socio-Economic Development. Twenty-six of the twenty-seven companies were listed on the Tokyo Stock Exchange; the remaining firm was among the top ten in sales in its industrial group. The survey included extensive data on the impact that the companies' management reforms had had on life in the workplace and on the work and attitudes of individual employees.

The focal point was the question, "What impact has the introduction of a performance-based pay system had on your own incentive to work?" Responses were divided into three groups: "increased," "unchanged," or "decreased," and an attempt was made to discover which factors affected the probability of answering "increased." The analytical method was the probit model used in chapter 4. (For further details, see "Shokuba Kankyō no Henka to Hataraku Iyoku, Funiki no Henka" [Changes in the Workplace Environment and Changes in the Atmosphere and the Incentive to Work], a joint study by Kambayashi Ryō, Shinozaki Takehisa, and me in *Shokuba to Kigyō no Rōshi Kankei no Saikōchiku* [Rebuilding Labour-Management Relations in the Workplace and the Company] [Japan Productivity Center for Socio-Economic Development, June 1999]; and "Seikashugi to Nōryoku Kaihatsu—Kekka toshite no Rōdō Iyoku" [Performance-based Systems + Skill Development = The Incentive to Work], another joint study by

**Table 6-2 Percentage by Which the Incentive to Work Increased with the Introduction of a Performance-Based Pay System**

| | All white collar workers (except those in management positions) | |
|---|---|---|
| Independent variables | Coefficient | IVi=1(%) IVi=3(%) |
| Workload for which one is responsible<br>1. decreased 2. unchanged 3. increased | 0.0354<br>(0.39) | −1.0<br>1.1 |
| Scope of the job<br>1. decreased 2. unchanged 3. increased | 0.1139<br>(1.90) | −3.2<br>3.5 |
| Scope entrusted to one's own discretion<br>1. decreased 2. unchanged 3. increased | 0.2605<br>(2.89) *** | −6.9<br>8.5 |
| Working hours<br>1. decreased 2. unchanged 3. increased | −0.1026<br>(−1.46) | 3.2<br>−2.9 |
| Job assignment, duties<br>1. less clear 2. unchanged 3. clearer | 0.2231<br>(3.57) *** | −6.0<br>7.2 |
| Responsibility<br>1. decreased 2. unchanged 3. increased | 0.0378<br>(0.39) | −1.1<br>1.1 |
| Performance<br>1. not strictly accountable 2. unchanged 3. strictly accountable | 0.1796<br>(2.25) ** | −5.0<br>5.7 |
| Job-related skills and knowledge<br>1. decreased 2. unchanged 3. increased | 0.0248<br>(0.22) | −0.7<br>0.7 |
| Opportunity to develop job-related skills<br>1. decreased 2. unchanged 3. increased | 0.3457<br>(4.99) *** | −8.9<br>11.5 |
| Constant | −3.0038<br>(−6.96) *** | |
| rho | −0.4974<br>(0.01) *** | |
| (Prob > $\chi^2$) | 0.00 | |
| Likelihood | −1521.47 | |
| Sample size | 1,606 | |
| Censor observattion | 1,070 | |

*Source:* Genda Yūji, Kambayashi Ryō, and Shinozaki Takehisa, "Seikashugi to Nōryoku Kaihatsu—Kekka toshite no Rōdō Iyoku" (Performance-based Systems + Skill Development = The Incentive to Work), *Soshiki Kagaku* (Organizational Science) 34, no. 3 (2001).

*Note:* Asymptotic t- values are given in parentheses. *** = significant at the 1% level; ** = significant at the 5% level; * = significant at the 10% level. The greater the number of asterisks, the more statistically reliable are the results.

the three of us in *Soshiki Kagaku* [Organizational Science] 34, no. 3 [2001].)

The results are found in table 6-2. To explain how to read this table, a positive number of 0.2231 is reported for the item "job assignment, duties." This means that respondents whose job assignment and duties had gone from being unclear to being clear had an increased probability of answering that a performance-based pay system has had a positive effect on their incentive to work (i.e., it went up). The asterisks here indicate that the result has a statistically high level of reliability. This reliability is judged by the asymptotic t-value given in parentheses. For example, even though the item "workload for which one is responsible" has a positive number of 0.0354, the t-value is much less than two. From this, it can be concluded that the reliability is low and that an increase or decrease in the workload per se is unrelated to the incentive to work.

What *does* stimulate the incentive to work are situations in which the job description changes, i.e., when the scope entrusted to one's own discretion increases, when the work assignments are clarified, when one is held strictly accountable for the performance of one's job, and when opportunities to develop skills increase. In the main text, I called these situations "improvements to the functional conditions of the job." Which of these functional conditions have a particularly strong impact on work incentive? At the far right of the table, two numbers are given for each item. In the case of "scope entrusted to one's own discretion," for example, the numbers are minus 6.9 and 8.5. These figures mean that, at the average white collar workplace where a performance-based system has been introduced, there is an 8.5 percent rise in the probability that the incentive to work will go up when the scope for independent action increases, and a 6.9 percent decline when it decreases.

If shifting to a salary system that gives greater weight to results and outcomes is to increase the incentive to work and not detract from it, improvements will need to be made concurrently to such functional conditions as clarifying job assignments and reviewing the scope given to employees to use their own initiative. The difficulty of evaluating results has been pointed out as one of the problems with introducing a performance-based system. Clarifying job assignments subject to evaluation and expanding the scope entrusted to the employee's discretion will be important points in facilitating a boss's evaluation process.

The functional condition that has an even greater effect than these two items on boosting the incentive to work is increasing the opportunity to develop job-related skills. From the right side of the table we can see that, if opportunities to develop skills increase concurrently with the introduction of a performance-based system, the probability of an improvement in the incentive to work goes up 11.5 percent. The degree of increase is far greater than for any other item. Conversely, when a performance-based system is introduced, and opportunities to develop skills decrease, the probability of an improvement in work incentive goes down 8.9 percent.

The opportunity to develop skills has a stronger impact than other functional conditions on the incentive to work. If a change in the salary system leads to an emphasis on short-term results and opportunities to develop long-term skills are reduced, the probability of an increased work incentive will go down, and this in turn will ultimately lead to a decline in productivity. For that very reason, if a performance-based system is to succeed, it will be important to clarify job descriptions and expand the opportunities for employees to develop their skills.

# *Chapter 7*

# *Conditions for a happy job change*

## Why job changes among middle-aged and older workers are unhappy

"Mobility" is a concept that is hard for Japanese to like. It implies that moving from one job and to another is part of the natural order, but, even if that were the case, the reasons for making such a move vary from person to person: some have found a better job; others have been forced to seek new employment when their company has gone bankrupt; some would just like to quit their present job; others have quit for no reason. If all these utterly different motives for switching jobs are lumped together under the term "mobility," the discussion about whether the Japanese labour market should be more mobile loses its focus.

For most people changing jobs is not a simple matter. For middle-aged and older workers, in particular, their age is a problem. The debate over prohibiting age-related discrimination is not confined to the issue of what to do about the mandatory retirement system. An even bigger concern is whether or not it is appropriate to specify age limits for job openings. The main reason that middle-aged and older workers have so little success finding new jobs is that their age does not match the age profile for the position being advertised. According to the *Report on the Special Survey of the Labour Force* (August 2000) carried out by the Statistics Bureau of the Management and Coordination Agency, nearly forty percent of the unemployed aged forty-five to fifty-four and half of those aged fifty-five to sixty-four failed to get a position because they were deemed too old for the job. As of October 2001, the law has been amended in an effort to eliminate age limits related to hiring and recruitment.

But even though setting age limits for job vacancies has been banned on the grounds of ageism, unfortunately, that does not mean that employment prospects for middle-aged and older workers will suddenly improve. The enactment of the Equal Opportunity Law may have made it illegal to specify gender in help wanted ads, but during the bleak job market for new graduates in the early 1990s, women had a much harder time finding a job than men did. It would be a different story if companies had been blatantly discriminatory and refused to interview female applicants, but the fact is that companies basically prefer to hire men who are young and who will work for them for a long time and that tendency remains unchanged. In the absence of any clear criteria other than age to indicate an applicant's ability, the prospects of finding a new job will remain as dismal as ever for middle-aged and older workers.

Are certified skills what middle-aged and older workers need to solve the job change dilemma? Certification is certainly one way of demonstrating proficiency, but the truth of the matter is that workers who only have paper credentials and nothing else to prove their skills have a hard time getting a job. Most corporate personnel managers say that, while having certified skills is invaluable, in all but a few occupational categories they are not the determining factor. What, then, is important for middle-aged and older workers who are looking for new jobs? Ultimately, it boils down to the sort of work they did at their previous place of employment. Unless they have specialized skills or transferable skills that are applicable at any company, switching jobs, it is said, will be difficult.

As counterpoint to all the brave talk about a new age of professionalism, the following funny story has been making the rounds. At an interview for a new job, a businessman was asked, "What sort of work can you do?" "Anything along the line of section chief," he replied. But it is no joke. Even in this day and age, there are still people who have nothing but their title to rely on. On the other hand, many section chiefs who do have ability and are good at their jobs are nevertheless unable to articulate to the outside world what it is they do. Information about an individual's work habits circulates within the company, but take one step outside, and most of us have never talked about our jobs—and have never been asked about them either. The tragic result of this situation is the punch line, "Anything along the line of section chief." Whether as part of a job search or within our own firms, each of us needs to have a little pride and confidence in the work we do and be able to describe it in our own words.

Even if job change becomes more common, it doesn't mean that everyone will achieve greater satisfaction as a result. Job change under any circumstances always involves some degree of uncertainty. There will always be those who are happy with their new jobs and those who are not. Individuals who improve their circumstances by taking the risk and changing jobs share certain characteristics. What is it that distinguishes a happy job change from an unhappy one?

## Stayers and leavers

Deep down, what differentiates those who leave their jobs and move on to another one from those who do not? Let us focus on college graduates or those with advanced degrees below the age of sixty who quit their jobs (let's call them "leavers") and those who did not ("stayers") and look at the differences between them both at home and at work.

What is striking first of all about the characteristics summed up in table 7-1 is age distribution and company size. The average age of the leavers is 41.1; 29.7 percent are in their forties, 23.4 percent are in their fifties; those two age groups account for more than half the total. On the other hand, the average age of the stayers is 35.4, five years younger than the leavers; 38.0 percent are under thirty, 30.7 percent are in their thirties, and the percentage of those over forty is relatively low. When we look at company size (the number of full-time regular employees working at the company as a whole), the percentage of stayers who work at large companies with more than 1,000 employees is overwhelmingly high—around fifty-five percent. Only around eleven percent of the leavers work for companies with more than 1,000 employees. In the case of leavers who are college graduates, it is the general practice to get a job at a large company immediately after graduation, then to switch to a

**Table 7-1 Stayers and Leavers who Are College Graduates (or have advanced degrees) and Are Currently Working as Full-Time Regular Employees**

| | Stayers | Leavers |
|---|---|---|
| Have you ever changed jobs? | no | yes |
| Breakdown (%) | | |
| Gender | | |
| Male | 85.5 | 83.4 |
| Female | 14.5 | 16.6 |
| Highest level of schooling | | |
| College graduate | 95.2 | 96.3 |
| Advanced degree | 4.8 | 3.8 |
| Age distribution | | |
| Under 30 | 38.0 | 15.0 |
| 30–39 | 30.7 | 31.9 |
| 40–49 | 21.1 | 29.7 |
| 50 or over | 10.2 | 23.4 |
| Average age | 35.4 | 41.1 |
| Company size (number of employees) | | |
| 1–29 | 7.8 | 28.8 |
| 30–99 | 7.2 | 18.1 |
| 100–299 | 12.7 | 24.7 |
| 300–999 | 17.5 | 15.9 |
| 1,000–4,999 | 31.3 | 7.8 |
| 5,000 or more | 23.5 | 3.4 |
| Uncertain | 0.0 | 1.3 |

*Note*: All tables and figures in chapter 7 are cited from Genda Yūji, "'Kōfuku na Tenshoku' no J ken" (Conditions for a 'Successful Job Change'), *JILI Forum*, no. 10 (2001), Seimei Hoken Bunka Center. The sample surveyed consisted of 166 stayers and 320 leavers; leavers figure more prominently in the surveyed data.

smaller firm. The data show that just over seventy percent of the leavers are now working for small or medium-sized companies with fewer than 300 employees.

Table 7-2 looks at the difference between stayers and leavers regarding their attitudes toward work. More stayers than leavers responded that they are "satisfied" or "fairly satisfied" with their present job and place of employment, perhaps reflecting the fact that a higher percentage of them work for large companies where salary and other working conditions are relatively good. Had they been extremely dissatisfied, presumably they would have already quit. Among leavers, who are

**Table 7-2 Attitudes toward Work**

| | Stayers | Leavers |
|---|---|---|
| Overall level of satisfaction (%) | | |
| Satisfied | 10.8 | 10.0 |
| Fairly satisfied | 45.2 | 40.0 |
| Neither satisfied nor dissatisfied | 25.9 | 23.8 |
| Fairly dissatisfied | 12.7 | 14.4 |
| Dissatisfied | 5.4 | 10.6 |
| Uncertain | 0.0 | 1.3 |
| Percentage who wish to change employer, change profession, or go into business for oneself (%) | | |
| Wish to change employer | 26.5 | 28.8 |
| Wish to change profession | 1.2 | 2.8 |
| Wish to go into business for oneself | 9.0 | 17.8 |
| Do not want to change employer, change profession, or go into business for oneself | 63.3 | 49.1 |
| Uncertain | 0.0 | 1.6 |
| Percentage who have taken courses to upgrade their skills (%) | | |
| Have not | 62.7 | 61.3 |
| Have | 37.4 | 38.8 |
| Average amount of money spent in the last year on courses to upgrade one's skills (1,000 yen) | 63.4 | 86.3 |
| Until what age do you think you would like to work? | | |
| Average age | 60.7 | 62.9 |
| Median age | 60 | 65 |

thought to have changed jobs in search of a better place of employment, as many as 10.6 percent responded that they are "dissatisfied" and 14.4 percent responded that they are "fairly dissatisfied" with their new jobs, higher percentages than for stayers.

What are some of the specific differences between stayers and leavers in what they found satisfying about their jobs or place of employment? A glance at figure 7-1 shows that the overwhelming majority of stayers, 48.8 percent, cited "employment stability." By contrast, an equally high percentage of leavers, most of whom tend to work at small and medium-sized firms, cite "type of work" as the reason for their satisfaction. Leavers are also more likely than stayers to cite "opportunity to demonstrate one's skills" and "company's future prospects." A profile of leavers is beginning to emerge: they give higher priority to the kind of work they do than to

**Fig. 7-1 Aspects of Your Present Job or Place of Employment That Are Satisfying** (multiple responses)

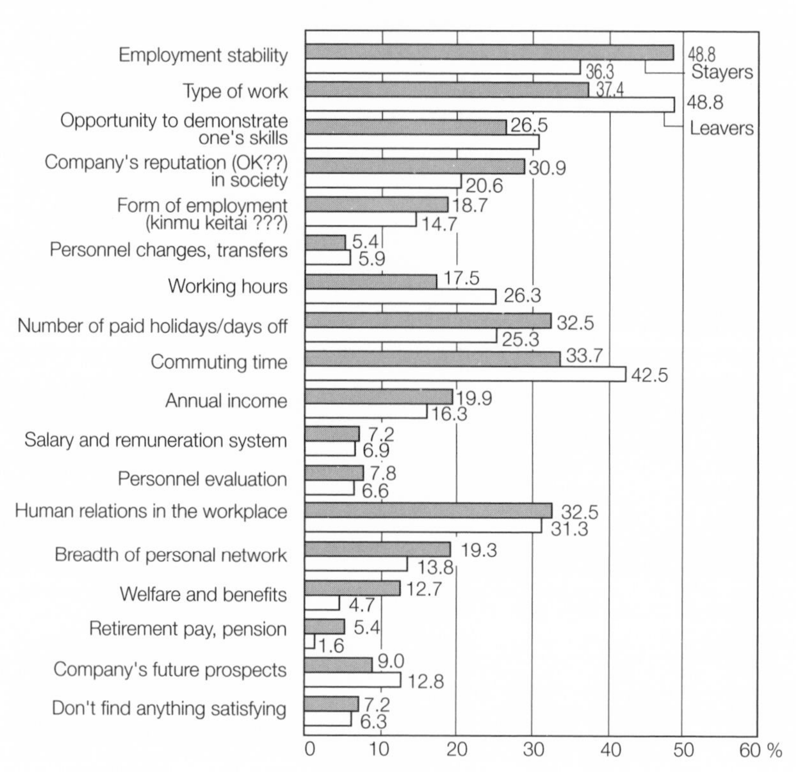


job security. More leavers than stayers cite "commuting time" as one of their reasons for being satisfied with their new job; quite a few changed jobs for convenience' sake or to achieve a better balance between their work and family life.

Returning once more to table 7-2, let us consider the respondents' desire to change their employer or their profession or to set up their own business. Almost twice the number of leavers than stayers—17.8 percent—contemplate going into business for themselves someday. On the other hand, 63.3 percent of the stayers have no plans whatsoever to change their employer or profession or to open their own business. Despite all the talk about the mobility of the labour market, most people still want to spend their working life at a single company.

As for future skill development, it is often said that instead of companies taking the lead, it will be important for workers to come to grips with this issue on their own initiative. There is no big difference between stayers and leavers when it comes to self-education (studies aimed at improving their job-related skills or knowledge or at acquiring officially recognized accreditation or skills). In terms of the amount of money spent on self-education during the past year, however, leavers outspent stayers by more than 20,000 yen: 86,000 yen on average as opposed to 63,000 yen. In order to get a better job, leavers invest aggressively in their own education.

Nor do leavers lag behind stayers when it comes to attitudes toward work in the future. When asked, "Until what age would you like to work?" leavers hope to work longer than stayers. Their desired retirement age is 62.9 on average versus 60.7 for stayers. The median age (the exact halfway point) is sixty for stayers and sixty-five for leavers. Leavers are strongly work oriented, and for that reason alone they tend to be dissatisfied, but most of them seem to want to have a job they really enjoy and to make use of their skills over a long period of time.

## Stayers' and leavers' outlook on life

To look at this point from a different angle, let us shift our focus to the plans that stayers and leavers have made for their futures. Unlike 69.9 percent of the stayers, only 55.9 percent of the leavers have made no plans for their future work life, i.e., finding a new job, starting their own business or retiring. Leavers are much more likely than stayers to have plans and strong feelings about the work they want to do in the future and how they want to do it. On the other hand, a majority of leavers (53.4 percent) "have made no plans" for life events (getting married, having a child, buying a house, etc.). More than 60 percent of the stayers, on the other hand, have some sort of plan for these events. If leavers can be described as job oriented or work oriented, then, stayers have a strong tendency to be life-event oriented.

These different tendencies are also found in stayers' and leavers' home life. The decision to marry, have a child, or buy a home is affected by the stage a person is at in his/her life plan. As we saw in table 7-1, there is a significant difference in the age distribution of stayers and leavers. Accordingly, let us limit our comparison to the domestic circumstances of male stayers and leavers in their thirties and forties. Table 7-3 shows that, among respondents as a whole, a higher percentage of leavers than stayers are married. This reflects the difference in age distribution. If we look at men between the ages of thirty and forty-nine, however, the percentage of those who have never married is 1.2 among stayers but a high as 11.3 among leavers; in addition, more stayers than leavers have children.

Among respondents as a whole, a higher percentage of leavers own their own home. But this, too, is affected by the difference in age distribution; among men in the thirty-to-forty-nine age range, the percentage of home owners is higher among stayers. In particular, the number of home owners making mortgage payments is nearly five percent higher among stayers than among leavers. Since paying off a mortgage requires a steady income, home ownership deters people from changing jobs and incurring the risk of income fluctuations. Another special feature related to housing is shared both by men between thirty and forty-nine and by respondents as a whole: the percentage of stayers who live in housing owned or leased by their companies or in bachelor dormitories was more than ten percent higher than for leavers, many of whom live in rental housing. The large companies where most stayers work provide a full range of housing facilities; stayers, it would seem, also avoid changing jobs because it means relinquishing their housing privileges.

Spouses are another area in which stayers and leavers differ. More than sixty percent of the spouses of stayers are full-time homemakers. In fact, that figure is nearly seventy percent for stayers aged thirty-to-forty-nine. Both these figures are ten percent higher than for spouses of leavers. Husbands who are college graduates get a job at a large company and stay there, drawing in a secure salary while their wives stay at home looking after the family; it is they who take primary responsibility for seeing to it that their family achieves its life plan. By contrast, a high percentage of the spouses of leavers are full-time employees at private-sector firms or work at part-time or temporary jobs.

## Table 7-3 Domestic Circumstances (%)

| | All Respondents | | Men aged 30–49 | |
|---|---|---|---|---|
| | Stayers | Leavers | Stayers | Leavers |
| Marital circumstances | | | | |
| Married (first marriage) | 65.7 | 73.4 | 92.8 | 82.1 |
| Married (remarried) | 3.0 | 2.2 | 3.6 | 3.6 |
| Married (divorced or widowed) | 0.0 | 3.1 | 0.0 | 1.2 |
| Not married | 29.5 | 18.8 | 1.2 | 11.3 |
| Children | | | | |
| Have children | 84.2 | 83.3 | 88.8 | 85.6 |
| Do not have children | 15.8 | 16.7 | 11.3 | 14.4 |
| Housing | | | | |
| Own home (paying mortgage) | 27.1 | 33.4 | 42.2 | 37.5 |
| Own home (no mortgage or mortgage paid up) | 10.8 | 15.9 | 10.8 | 9.5 |
| Live with parents in their home | 22.3 | 20.9 | 12.1 | 19.1 |
| Rental housing | 22.3 | 25.3 | 18.1 | 27.4 |
| Housing owned or leased by company, bachelor dormitory | 17.5 | 4.1 | 16.9 | 6.6 |
| Employment status of spouse | | | | |
| Full-time employee at private sector company | 11.4 | 14.9 | 6.3 | 7.6 |
| Government employee | 1.8 | 2.5 | 0.0 | 1.4 |
| Dispatched worker, contract worker | 0.0 | 3.3 | 0.0 | 2.8 |
| Does part-time or temporary work | 19.3 | 23.6 | 22.5 | 24.3 |
| Domestic help | 0.9 | 2.1 | 0.0 | 2.1 |
| Liberal profession | 1.8 | 0.4 | 1.3 | 0.7 |
| Stay-at-home homemaker | 64.0 | 48.8 | 68.8 | 56.9 |
| Satisfaction with family life | | | | |
| Satisfied | 26.5 | 24.4 | 31.3 | 26.2 |
| Fairly satisfied | 48.2 | 53.1 | 45.8 | 53.0 |
| Neither satisfied nor dissatisfied | 21.7 | 14.7 | 20.5 | 14.9 |
| Fairly dissatisfied | 2.4 | 6.6 | 2.4 | 5.4 |
| Dissatisfied | 1.2 | 0.9 | 0.0 | 0.0 |
| Uncertain | 0.0 | 0.3 | 0.0 | 0.6 |

*Note*: Some numbers do not total 100% either out of uncertainty or as a result of rounding off.

Leavers' earnings as a percentage of their total household finances also have an effect on the reason their spouses work. A glance at median annual incomes given in table 7-4 shows that, both among all respondents and among males between the ages of thirty and forty-nine, stayers make a million yen more than leavers. As for the average annual

**Table 7-4 Economic Conditions**

| | All Respondents | | Men aged 30–49 | |
|---|---|---|---|---|
| | Stayers | Leavers | Stayers | Leavers |
| (1) Annual income (respondent) | | | | |
| Average (10,000 yen) | 629.0 | 583.3 | 737.2 | 619.6 |
| Median (10,000 yen) | 600 | 500 | 700 | 600 |
| (2) Annual income (total for respondent and spouse) | | | | |
| Average (10,000 yen) | 700.4 | 668.0 | 772.5 | 675.5 |
| Median (10,000 yen) | 650 | 600 | 720 | 637.5 |
| (3) Total amount of savings, cash value life insurance, and investments | | | | |
| Average (million yen) | 107.1 | 134.6 | 96.5 | 109.8 |
| Median (million yen) | 100 | 100 | 100 | 100 |
| percentage savings | 67.6 | 57.9 | 58.6 | 57.1 |
| percentage cash value life insurance | 26.0 | 31.8 | 35.7 | 33.6 |
| percentage investments | 6.5 | 10.3 | 5.7 | 9.2 |
| (4) Average propensity to save (= (3)/(2)) | | | | |
| Average | 0.163 | 0.198 | 0.128 | 0.157 |
| Median | 0.133 | 0.143 | 0.117 | 0.126 |
| (5) Total monetary assets | | | | |
| Average (10,000 yen) | 758.7 | 1099.3 | 956.2 | 963.0 |
| Median (10,000 yen) | 500 | 500 | 500 | 500 |
| (6) Monthly living expenses (including rent or mortgage payments) | | | | |
| Average (10,000 yen) | 27.4 | 28.9 | 30.1 | 28.5 |
| Median (10,000 yen) | 25 | 28 | 29 | 25 |

*Note*: When the entry for spouse's salary was left blank, it was calculated as zero.

income for men in the thirty-to-forty-nine age group, here, too, stayers outearn leavers by more than a million yen. When spousal income is added, however, the gap between the two groups shrinks, reflecting the high spousal employment rate in leavers' households. Yet, even so, there is a gap in both the average and median annual income of between 500,000 and a million yen.

While stayers may have higher incomes, leavers and their spouses saved and invested more during the preceding year. On average, they and their spouses save or invest around three percent more of their total annual income than stayers and their spouses do. Because leavers face a high risk of fluctuating incomes, their households channel a high percentage of their income into savings in the hope of stabilizing their livelihood. In the households of stayers, a high percentage of all their money and investments goes into stable assets such as bank accounts (regular and term deposits, company savings plans, etc.). In leavers' households, on the other hand, approximately ten percent goes into investments (government bonds, stock, investment trusts, money market funds, midium-term government bond funds, foreign currency deposit accounts, etc.). They have a stronger propensity for risk than the more stability-minded stayer households. But despite their different orientations toward saving and investing, no conspicuous difference can be found in the two groups' total financial assets. For both respondents as a whole and for men aged thirty to forty-nine, the median is five million yen, and the average for both stayers and leavers among men aged thirty to forty-nine is around 9.5 million.

The difference is far greater when it comes to daily living expenses (including rent and mortgage payments). Among all respondents, living expenses are higher for leavers than for stayers, but here, too, age distribution has an effect. When restricted to men aged thirty to forty-nine, both median and average living expenses are higher for stayers than for leavers. Because stayers have more income, they can afford to direct more of their money into the purchase of consumer goods and consumer durables; at the same time, a large portion goes into paying off their housing loans. From this too, we can tell that the career decision to stay or to leave has an effect on the way a family lives as well as on the way it spends and saves its money.

Generally speaking, what sort of image emerges from the above information? Table 7-5 ventures to sum up the characteristics of the two groups. In terms of what they consider important in life, stayers are strongly "family oriented"; they are also "stability oriented" in the face of uncertainty. Because they value security above all, they continue to work at the large companies where they were first employed. Their ideal is to work until retirement at age sixty and then live a carefree retired life. Since their first consideration is their families, they either buy their own home or live in company-owned housing and live an affluent consumer life style spending what remains. Household management is the role of their wives, who are stay-at-home housewives; they are risk

**Table 7-5 Typical Model of Leavers and Stayers among College Graduates and those with Advanced Degrees**

| | Item | Stayer | Leaver |
|---|---|---|---|
| Attitudes, values | What do you consider important? | Family oriented | Work oriented |
| | Attitude toward certainty | Security oriented | Risk taker |
| Work conditions | Salary | Large salary | Small salary |
| | Place of employment | Works for a large company | Works for a small or medium-sized company |
| | Present job | More or less satisfied | Dissatisfied |
| | Future job | Content with what I'm doing now | Considering starting own business |
| | Date of retirement | Would like to work until age 60 | Would like to work until age 65 |
| Domestic circumstances | Spouse | Stay-at-home housewife | Employed |
| | Housing | Company housing or owns own home | Rental housing |
| | Consumption and savings | Consumption oriented | Savings oriented |
| | Means of asset formation | Primarily savings | Savings and investments |

averse even when it comes to asset formation, primarily putting their money in term deposits and other kinds of bank accounts.

By contrast, leavers are strongly "work oriented" and want a job that will make the best use of their talents; they are risk takers who do not mind uncertainty and are even willing to take a pay cut for the right job. Because they are strongly focused on their work, there is much they are dissatisfied about. Nevertheless, they want to work for a long time to come and even have hopes of opening their own business some day. Since they work at small and mid-sized companies, they don't earn much, but because their wives work too, their income helps to make up the difference. They have a high propensity to save, and in many cases they invest as part of their asset formation. They do not necessarily have a strong desire to own their own home and are satisfied with rental housing. This is the image of a typical leaver and his household.

The reason I have attempted to make composite images such as these is that, as I mentioned at the start of this chapter, I wanted to confirm once again that it is impossible to say whether it is good or bad that mobility is leading to an increase in the number of job changes. The underlying belief among those who do not change jobs but continue to work for a single company is the idea that their family comes first. Far be it from me to deny the importance of that. On the other hand, in most cases, leavers did not quit their jobs because they were bored with their work; rather, quite the opposite, they decide to leave because their focus on their work is so strong.

Most people in their teens and twenties think that being able to work as a full-time employee at a single company is the best choice for their future development. For those in their thirties and forties, however, the decision to quit or to stay is greatly affected by their individual attitudes about work and family. It is wrong to lump all such people together when debating the pros and cons of mobility.

## The key to a happy job change

If I were to venture to narrow down what characterizes a disparate group of leavers, it is that they are work oriented and risk takers. When it comes to taking risks, personal temperament is a big factor. But for the person who, despite the uncertainty, decides to quit one job and take another, isn't there something else that is even more important: being able to envision the possibility of success?

At the very least, there is something that leads a person to take the risk and change jobs in order to improve his/her situation. What sort of person takes up that risky challenge and feels that the change was, in fact, a success. What are the conditions for a happy job change? The results below are shocking. Why? Because no matter how much the government or the private sector may invest in upgrading their job placement agencies, such services cannot necessarily be said to make for successful job changes. And no matter how much a person may work to upgrade his/her skills, that alone does not lead to a happy job change either. Is it family or relatives, then, that are important? What about deep human relations built up among colleagues? None of the above.

What is important is whether or not one has trustworthy friends and acquaintances outside the workplace.

Figure 7-2 shows in graph form the percent who were satisfied with their new company, whose salary improved and whose working hours and days off were better as a result of a job change. It contains the results of calculations to determine how much these percentages differed for those who answered yes or no to the question "Did you have friends or acquaintances outside the workplace who gave you valuable advice at the time of job change?" Of course, these percentages are also affected by age and gender. Here the influence of friends and acquaintances is studied in greater depth once the impact of these other factors is removed. (For further details see "The data Speak" at the end of the chapter.) A glance at the figure shows that only thirty-eight percent of those who did not have friends or acquaintances outside the workplace to give them useful advice at the time of job change responded that their level of satisfaction was higher at their new job than it had been at their former company, as compared with forty-nine percent of those who did, a difference of more than ten percent. In addition, eight-two percent who had friends or acquaintances outside the company said they had no regrets about joining their new firm. For those without such friends and acquaintances the number was only 58 percent.

Emotional satisfaction is not the only area in which the existence of friends and acquaintances outside the workplace looms large. It also plays an important role in improving the income of those who have found new jobs. The figure shows that, when a job changer does not have such friends or acquaintances, only forty-three percent reported that their salary conditions had improved. On the other hand, when a job changer does have friends and acquaintances who can give valuable advice, the majority (fifty-six percent) improved their earnings. It might be noted in passing that sevevty-eight percent of those who found jobs with the aid of a headhunter reported an improvement in income. Although not as high as a headhunter, friends and acquaintances have a great effect on finding a place of employment with better salary conditions. Friends also make for a happy job change in areas other than income. About one in two job changers who had friends they could consult outside the workplace replied that their working hours and days off are better than they

**Fig. 7-2 Presence or Absence of Friends and Acquaintances Outside the Workplace Who Can Give Advice at the Time of Job Change and Post-Change Conditions**

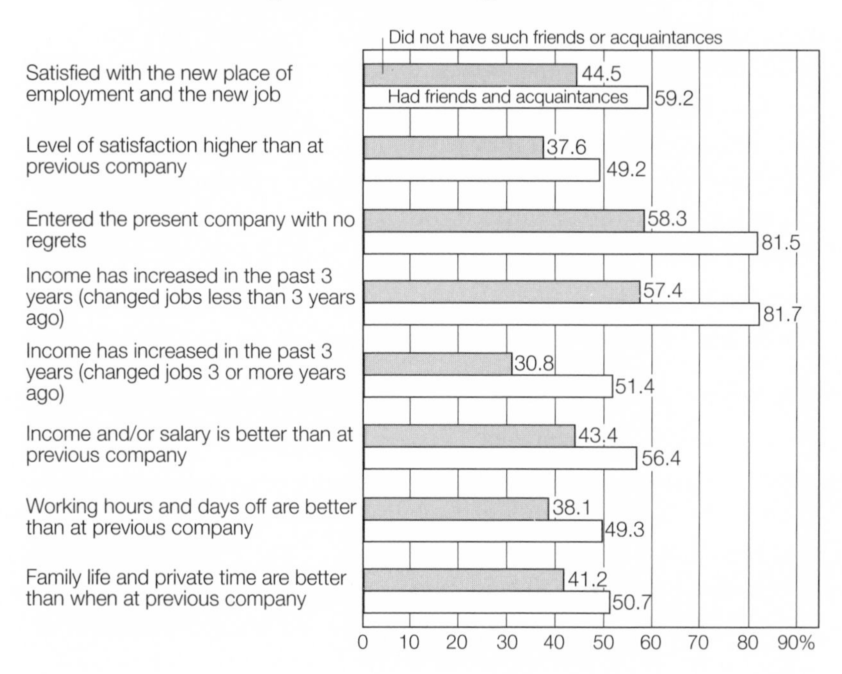


had been at their previous company. By contrast, just under forty percent of those without such friends and acquaintances said their working hours had improved. Thus, there is nearly a ten percent difference between the two groups in terms of increased family time and private time. Having friends and acquaintances outside the workplace, then, is a prerequisite for a high level of overall satisfaction with one's new job; in other words, it is key to a happy job change.

Although not shown on the figure, another important discovery can be drawn from these data. It has to do with what sort of people think they might like to start their own business someday. Surprisingly, here, too, the determinant for an entrepreneurial spirit is whether or not one has friends with whom one can consult. The data for those who have changed jobs and those who have not were used to calculate the probability that they might want to own their own business someday. Those who answered "friend or acquaintance outside the workplace" to the question "if you were planning to change jobs (or look for a job), change professions, or start your own business, whom would you consult?" (multiple choices) were far more likely to say that they would like to go into business for themselves. Only 13.7 percent of those who did not have such friends or acquaintances—as opposed to 21.9 percent who did—answered that they would like to start their own business. Entrepreneurial individuals not only possess the personal attributes of abundant talent and an adventurous spirit; they also have friends and acquaintances they can consult.

## Human relations outside the workplace

Why is having trustworthy friends and acquaintances outside the workplace conducive to a happy job change? It is easy to imagine that such a friend or acquaintance may work at the company the prospective job changer is thinking of joining. If job leavers are able to talk frankly and thoroughly about working conditions and other concerns they might have with a friend who already works there, they are more likely to join the new firm with few regrets. They are far less likely to feel that the situation is not what they expected, if they have had the opportunity to talk things over thoroughly beforehand with a friend who works there. Such conversations can help prevent a job change that would probably turn out to be unsatisfactory. The possibility of a mismatch can largely be averted by having a friend or acquaintance at the company one is planning to join.

But even without being at the new company itself, a friend or acquaintance fulfills an important function in helping a potential job changer evaluate the information about the new job. The Japanese word *jōhō* consists of two characters, both of which mean "information" but whose connotations differ greatly. According to Ogawa Akira (*Hyōgen no Tatsujin, Settoku no Tatsujin* [Experts at Communication and Persuasion] [Tokyo: TBS-Britanika, 1991]), *hō* is publicly available information to which anyone who so desires can have access any time and anywhere, whereas *jō* implies inside information and/or nuances obtained only through face-to-face communication, i.e., information that can only be discovered and acquired firsthand.

Some quantitative information such as salary levels and number of paid holidays is available at public and private job placement agencies. But trustworthy friends play a big role when it comes to judging subjective or qualitative information. This sort of information (e.g., how to evaluate working conditions at the firm one is hoping to join) is acquired through consulting and conferring with close friends. When the time comes to make a decision, subjective information is just as valuable as the objective kind. The importance of friends and acquaintances attests to the importance of subjective information in laying the psychological and emotional groundwork for making a job change.

By observing the job and work habits of a friend at a different workplace and projecting oneself onto him/her, a potential job changer imagines what it would be like to work there successfully. He/she judges from the work style of a friend whose personality and abilities are well known whether the job is something that "I can do too." Having a friend who can serve as a model provides input for making a cool-headed assessment about how one would fit into the new work environment. Thus, friends and acquaintances not only serve as a yardstick by which to compare one's own abilities, they are also an important factor in the decision-making process on an emotional level by providing sympathetic yet objective and unsentimental advice.

Without a friend or acquaintance to act as an adviser, it is impossible to make an objective assessment of the uncertainties of the job change. As a result, it is highly likely that one will not take the plunge, or, if one does, that the new job will not be satisfying. A friend and acquaintance one can trust, whom one meets occasionally outside the company, can turn the uncertainties of job change into risks. Their importance has also been noted in American studies. The sociologist Mark Granovetter in his book *Getting a Job* (Chicago: University of Chicago Press, 1995) writes that people making a job change are more likely to receive useful information from those with whom they have "weak ties" (those whom they meet infrequently) than from those with whom they have "strong ties" (those whom they see all the time), and that the use of personal connections is the most effective way to gather good reliable information and to cancel out the noise generated by the process of looking for a new job.

The reason for the emphasis on the role of weak ties is that we learn only what we already know from people we see all the time whereas friends we meet only occasionally are the source of new information. Thought of in this light, friends working at the same company who often go drinking together would be strong ties. But weak ties also fulfill an important role in a successful job change even in Japan.

## Between the individual and the community

The key to happiness in a new job is to have trustworthy friends and acquaintances outside the workplace. Advice provided by public or private job placement agencies or by relatives and/or colleagues at one's former company does not by itself make for a successful job change. By contrast, when one has friends and acquaintance outside the workplace whom one can consult, not only is one more likely to derive greater satisfaction from the job change on an emotional level, income and private time also tend to improve. Conversely, if there was no one outside the workplace to give valuable advice at the time of job change, the likelihood is high that both working conditions and the level of satisfaction are more likely to decline. The formation of wide-ranging yet casual human relations is indispensable for doing work that will be satisfying throughout one's life.

But the relationship that Japanese actually have with their friends and acquaintances is proceeding in the opposite direction from this. It is said of young people nowadays that the only important thing is themselves; they give no thought whatsoever to the inconvenience they may cause to others. When I see a group of young people behaving badly on a Sunday train, for example, it is hard to deny this sort of criticism. Still, I feel like saying, "wait a minute." For members of the older generation, the expression "don't cause inconvenience to others" means not offending people one does not know. Taking the train as our example again, it means refraining from behavior that other passengers who just happen to be on the same train would regard as noisy and disruptive. The younger generation uses the expression in a different sense, however. For, them not causing inconvenience to others means not wanting to be in the bad graces of close friends on their cellphone list with whom they are in frequent contact by phone and by e-mail. The same expression has totally opposite meanings for different generations.

The fact that an awareness of and consideration for other people living in the same society are weakening and are being replaced by a concern solely for those with whom one is in close contact is in itself neither good nor bad. It is safe to say that many Japanese, not just young people, are becoming more "local." Even for those who live and work in the most fashionable part of the city, the ideas that stick are local ones. By "local" I mean showing an interest only in those things with which one has a personal relationship and being concerned exclusively with one's own territory. To repeat, I do not think this trend is either good or bad. According to Murakami Ryū, it is extremely natural that the communal consciousness of the past should disintegrate as part of the economic growth process (*Koyō Mondai o Kangaeru—Keiki to Kojin no Kōfukukan* [Thinking about the Employment Issue: Prosperity and the Individual's Perception of Happiness] [Tokyo: Nihon Hōsō Shuppan Kyōkai, 1999], 94). An awareness of one's local roots provides a certain sense of security. Instead of aspiring to win out and become number one in a fiercely competitive community consisting of unspecified masses of people, you can live in a community consisting only of yourself and those close to you and mutually confirm that you are the only ones that matter. Here you can find proof of your existence.

Under these sorts of circumstances, I won't say all, but almost all of the human relations of today's youth tend to be strong ties, close local friends whom they meet frequently and with whom they are in constant contact by cellphone, rather than weak ties, friends they meet infrequently. But in order to free oneself from the nagging sense of insecurity caused by changing jobs, one must be aware of the local nature of one's human relationships and consider ways of escaping from it.

## A harsh conclusion?

People who leave one job and move on to another are risk takers. Despite the possibility that they will not find satisfaction or earn a high salary, they still go ahead and change their job and place of employment. A new job does not always bring happiness; many who take the plunge end up feeling they have made a mistake. Someone with a mortgage who puts his/her family first would be better off not even considering it. Only those who are focused on their work should go ahead and make the change.

What does one need to do to find happiness in a new job? Have as many trustworthy friends and acquaintances as possible outside the workplace. Without them one will not be able to find satisfaction at the new job, and one's income and private time will not improve. Whether or not there is an increase in the number of people who want to be independent and open their own business someday, will depend on more people having more friends and acquaintances outside the workplace with whom they can consult than is now the case.

The idea that job change will be unsuccessful without friends and acquaintances on whom one can rely may perhaps sound like a harsh conclusion. But, even if the government makes it a policy to upgrade job placement agencies and increase the sources of information on job openings, that does not mean that job changers' incomes and level of satisfaction will increase as a result. If one is to make a successful transition to a new job, or thinks one might want to own one's own business, it is no use looking to the government or to deregulation for help. The important thing is to acquire the ability to make the right choice from among an almost endless supply of information, and to do that one has to have friends and acquaintances on whom one can rely.

When companies go bankrupt, when recession or the extension of the mandatory retirement age cause employment opportunities to shrivel up for recent graduates who are unable to find satisfying work, job turnover will inevitably increase. When that happens, the security- and family-orientedness found among the stayers will no longer be tenable. If they are to obtain happy employment opportunities, they will need to form a wide human network that extends beyond their company or their own family circle.

For most people in their thirties or forties, the daily routine revolves around home and work. Making new relationships becomes harder and more onerous. Not doing so, however, may be an impediment to a potential future job change or to setting up one's own business. As a way of acquiring friends and acquaintances outside the company, in addition to relations of trust with clients and customers, afull range of opportunities to participate in volunteer work, nonprofit organizations, and community activities will be important for an individual's choice of appropriate employment.

The importance of having friends and acquaintances when finding a job or looking for a new one is not a phenomenon unique to Japanese society. But for a society that has regarded lifetime employment as natural, haven't we been somewhat remiss about building and maintaining a human network that extends beyond the workplace? Japanese society needs to become a connections society not in the sense of being closed or class-based but in the good sense of the term; such connections are indispensable for building a labour market with few mismatches.

## The data speak

### Finding a new job, going into business for oneself, and the importance of friends and acquaintances

The data used here are from a survey on the diversification of work styles and changes in life plans that the Seimei Hoken Bunka Center conducted in September and October 2000.

College graduates and those with advanced degrees were selected out from a general survey of male and female employees between the ages of eighteen and fifty-nine and divided into two groups: those who had experienced a job change and those who had not. An additional survey was then conducted on individuals now working in the private sector who had changed jobs one or more times in order to isolate the characteristics of those who stay at their jobs and those who leave. The job change survey contained many items not found in the general survey, making it possible to explore the distinguishing features of the job leavers.

The left hand side of figure 7-6 contains a breakdown of the factors affecting the probability someone would answer that he/she had made a satisfactory or relatively satisfactory transition to a new job in response to the question "How did you feel when you made the decision to change jobs?" Here, too, a probit model was used. When the numbers that correspond to the explanatory variables on the far left are positive, the probability of satisfaction increases; it diminishes when they are negative. These figures are not actually zero, however; in other words, here, too, only the plus and minus numbers that have one, two or three asterisks next to them are statistically reliable. The greater the number of asterisks the higher the degree of reliability; such an item is definitely thought to have had an effect. Conversely, the probability of satisfaction is neither high nor low if there are no asterisks; in short, the absence of asterisks indicates that this particular variable has no effect. For example, the coefficient for "female" is minus 0.4322 with a single asterisk. This means that women have a lower likelihood of making a satisfactory transition to a new job than men do.

Among the factors affecting the degree of satisfaction with a job change, the response to the question, "Who gave you valuable advice when you moved to your present company?" (multiple responses) turned out to be particularly important. A glance at this shows that getting advice from private sector job placement agencies or headhunters did not lead to greater satisfaction. While some people were satisfied, many were not; no clear trends can be found. Similarly, when one's spouse, parents, close relatives, or other members of one's inner circle were the advisors, satisfaction with the job change did not go up. In the case of public job placement agencies (Hello Work, etc.), the probability of making a satisfactory job change actually went down; the figure was minus 0.4453 with one asterisk. This attests to the considerable difficulties facing those solitary souls who look for a job with only the advice of Hello Work to rely on.

The probability of a satisfied response is high for one item only: "friends and acquaintances outside the workplace." The coefficient is 0.7455 with three asterisks. When compiling a profile of the typical job changer, "marginal effect" is the degree to which a particular item affects probability. If the effect of other factors is excluded, the probability of a satisfied response was 0.2422, twenty-four percent higher for those who had friends and acquaintances to give them valuable advice than for those who did not.

We have looked at satisfaction resulting from job change, but what about income? The middle column of table 7-6 indicates fluctuations in income, i.e., results that enable us to judge whether or not earnings or income was better than at one's previous company. The probability of an improvement in income clearly diminishes for job changers fifty years old or older. Use of placement agencies, whether private or public, did not lead to a rise in salary, but, on the other hand, the advice of headhunters and spouses did. Although it seems reasonable that hiring a headhunter would lead to higher pay, are we to conclude that wives encourage their husbands to take jobs in which the conditions may be demanding but the compensation is better?

Here, too, the advice of friends and acquaintances outside the workplace helps improve working conditions after the job change. A look at the marginal effects shows that it accounts for a 15.77 percent rise in the

**Table 7-6 Effect of having Friends and Acquaintances Outside the Workplace on Satisfaction with One's New Job** (Probit model)

| | Estimated probability | Made transition to the new company with no regrets | | |
|---|---|---|---|---|
| Explanatory variables | | Coefficient | Z-value | Marginal effect |
| Age at the time of job change | Under 30 | 0.1279 | 0.59 | 0.0460 |
| | 40–49 | 0.0863 | 0.34 | 0.0310 |
| | 50 and over | -0.2325 | -0.91 | -0.0872 |
| Gender | Female | -0.4322 | -1.93* | -0.1642 |
| Highest level of education | Advanced degree | 0.0682 | 0.12 | 0.0244 |
| Past experience of job change | Employed twice in the past as a full-time employee | 0.3670 | 1.72* | 0.1296 |
| | Employed three times or more in the past as a full-time employee | -0.2481 | -1.13 | -0.0915 |
| Who gave valuable advice at the time of job change? | Public agency (Hello Work, etc.) | -0.4453 | -1.74* | -0.1706 |
| | Private job placement agency | 0.5643 | 1.48 | 0.1779 |
| | Headhunter | 0.7047 | 1.62 | 0.2123 |
| | Spouse | 0.2831 | 1.30 | 0.0988 |
| | Parent(s) | 0.3216 | 1.17 | 0.1098 |
| | Relatives and relations | 0.0096 | 0.03 | 0.0035 |
| | Boss | 0.2188 | 0.72 | 0.0763 |
| | Colleagues, staff, subordinates | 0.0988 | 0.22 | 0.0352 |
| | Friends and acquaintances outside the workplace | 0.7455 | 3.48*** | 0.2422 |
| | Teacher during one's student days | Not part of the sample | | |
| | Others | 0.3748 | 0.76 | 0.1243 |
| Points believed to have been evaluated at the time of job change | Previous work experience | 0.2380 | 0.86 | 0.0849 |
| | Personality and appearance | -0.0703 | -0.26 | -0.0257 |
| | Qualifications and skill | -0.0237 | -0.08 | -0.0086 |
| | Out of work due to bankruptcy of previous place of employment | -0.5229 | -1.48 | -0.2024 |
| | Number of years of service after job change | | | |
| | Constant | 0.0889 | 0.29 | |
| | Sample size | 284 | | |
| | Log likelihood | 47.25 | | |
| | Prob>$\chi^2$ | 0.0009 | | |
| | Pseudo $R^2$ | 0.1274 | | |

*Note*: *** = significant at the 1% level; ** = significant at the 5% level; * = significant at the 10% level; the Z-value is an asymptotic t-value

| Earnings and income were better than at previous company | | | Working hours and days off were better than at previous company | | |
|---|---|---|---|---|---|
| Coefficient | Z-value | Marginal effect | Coefficient | Z-value | Marginal effect |
| 0.2568 | 1.24 | 0.1019 | 0.2371 | 1.15 | 0.0922 |
| -0.2902 | -1.16 | -0.1127 | -0.3229 | -1.29 | -0.1195 |
| -0.7832 | -2.86*** | -0.2840 | -0.3231 | -1.24 | -0.1197 |
| 0.0896 | 0.40 | 0.0356 | -0.2990 | -1.29 | -0.1115 |
| 0.3039 | 0.55 | 0.1207 | -0.3212 | -0.60 | -0.1171 |
| 0.1168 | 0.54 | 0.0464 | -0.4718 | -2.20** | -0.1762 |
| 0.3235 | 1.46 | 0.1282 | -0.0101 | -0.05 | -0.0039 |
| -0.3558 | -1.31 | -0.1368 | 0.3017 | 1.12 | 0.1187 |
| 0.1518 | 0.43 | 0.0604 | -0.6956 | -1.82 | -0.2325 |
| 1.1435 | 2.91*** | 0.4044 | -0.6023 | -1.56 | -0.2068 |
| 0.5356 | 2.54** | 0.2112 | 0.1245 | 0.60 | 0.0487 |
| 0.1331 | 0.50 | 0.0529 | -0.0424 | -0.15 | -0.0162 |
| 0.1465 | 0.49 | 0.0583 | 0.2381 | 0.80 | 0.0935 |
| 0.1949 | 0.68 | 0.0775 | 0.1207 | 0.48 | 0.0470 |
| -0.0227 | -0.05 | -0.0090 | 0.3758 | 0.96 | 0.1484 |
| 0.3981 | 2.08** | 0.1577 | 0.3785 | 2.03** | 0.1480 |
| 0.0921 | 0.15 | 0.0366 | Not part of the sample | | |
| -1.1116 | -1.66* | -0.3526 | -0.3806 | -0.80 | -0.1371 |
| -0.3094 | -1.12 | -0.1213 | -0.3025 | -1.14 | -0.1144 |
| -0.0098 | -0.04 | -0.0039 | -0.4639 | -1.81* | -0.1725 |
| 0.0174 | 0.06 | 0.0069 | -0.7083 | -2.53** | -0.2495 |
| -0.4104 | -1.00 | -0.1557 | -0.2863 | -0.77 | -0.1055 |
| 0.0558 | 2.83*** | 0.0221 | 0.0176 | 0.94 | 0.0067 |
| -0.6029 | -1.88* | | 0.2100 | 0.67 | |
| | 287 | | | 280 | |
| | 63.48 | | | 36.13 | |
| | 0.000 | | | 0.0294 | |
| | 0.1601 | | | 0.0955 | |

probability that salary and income will improve. Having friends and acquaintances who can give advice contributes not just to a better salary but to other improvements in working conditions.

The right-hand side of table 7-6 shows the results of calculating the probability that working hours and days off would be better at the new company than at the old one. The probability that working hours, days off and private time will be better than they had been at one's previous job diminishes when evaluations are made of a worker's personality and appearance or his/her qualifications and skills. Working hours and days off are also less likely to improve when one finds a new job through a private job placement agency or when one changes a full-time job for the second time. Job change through a headhunter or for those in their forties is not linked to an improvement in private time. Here, too, the only item that is related to both improved working hours and days off and to an improvement in home life and private time is having friends and acquaintances outside the workplace. Judging from the marginal effect, the existence of such friends and acquaintances increases the probability that working conditions will improve by 14.8 percent.

Thus, the data attest to the conclusion that the condition for a happy job change is to have friends and acquaintances outside the workplace who can provide valuable advice.

# *Chapter 8*

# *Becoming One's Own Boss*

## A way for freeters to earn a living

Even supposing that young people's attitudes toward work have actually changed, so long as the employment of middle-aged and older workers continues to receive special consideration, the youth unemployment rate will remain high, and the number of freeters will rise. And if legislation is introduced to extend the mandatory retirement age and make age discrimination illegal while other systems and the existing environment remain unchanged, then, job protection for middle-aged and older workers will continue to grow, and the number of freeters and unemployed will increase even further.

There has been a growing debate recently over the right of dismissal. If the rules for terminating an employment relationship were to be changed and such matters as financial compensation for laid-off workers were clarified, this would also have an effect on youth employment. But, in fact, opposition to reviewing the right of dismissal is deep rooted. As Japanese society ages, preserving the jobs of middle-aged and older workers becomes more and more of an entrenched vested right. If no progress is made in reviewing the rules governing the employment relationship, what holds the key to expanding job opportunities and skill development opportunities for young people?

As outrageous as it may sound, I believe that perhaps the most important step for freeters is to set out on a path that will lead them to become a new type of independent business owner unlike anything that has ever been seen before. That means not being used as labour power, not having others decide what sort of work they should do. If freeters have the incentive to become their own boss, self-employment will increase as a result.

Has there been a rise, then, in the number of people who want to start their own businesses? The data exist to let us know the facts. And an altogether different picture of young people's attitudes toward self-employment emerges from the statistics. For many years, the *Employment Status Survey* has been calculating how many potential job changers want to go into business for themselves. Since young people have been shown to have a high propensity to switch jobs, if part of this job turnover can be attributed to a mounting interest in self-employment or in starting their own businesses, then the percentage of prospective job changers who hope to go into business for themselves should be on the rise. If we look at figure 8-1, however, the situation is the exact opposite. At the end of the 1970s, more than thirty percent of prospective job changers aged twenty-five to thirity four range wanted to open their own business. By the late 1980s, however, that figure was twenty-five percent, and, by the late 1990s, it had gone down even further to twenty percent. Similar declines occurred in the following two age ranges: from fifteen to twenty-four and from thirty-five to forty four.

On television and in magazines, the owner-managers of new venture businesses have been hailed as the heroes of our age. These standard bearers of venture capitalism are said to be the driving force behind the IT revolution and home care services. The young entrepreneurs spotlighted in these programs and articles are all articulate and brimming with self-confidence. But people like these are far removed from the realities that most Japanese young people face. The reason young people have no desire to be entrepreneurs is that, in today's difficult economic climate, it is becoming harder than ever before to run a business. Most people are well aware of that fact and have become increasingly cautious. Young people's appetite for risk has declined. One sign of this can be found in the steep decline in self-employment among those in their thirties and forties since the 1990s.

**Fig. 8-1 Percentage of Prospective Job Changers Who "Want to Be Their Own Boss"**

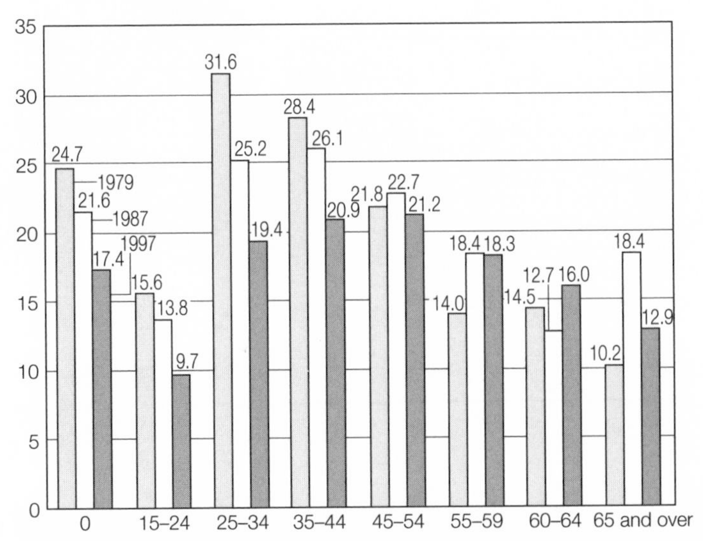


*Source*: Statistics Bureau, Management and Coordination Agency, *Employment Status Survey*

Figure 8-2 shows fluctuations in the number of self-employed according to age. For those in their fifties and sixties, the trend lines tend to level off or increase somewhat. For those in their thirties and forties, on the other hand, the decline has been noticeable since the late 1980s. As a result, in 1997, for the first time since 1970, self-employed persons in their fifties and sixties outnumbered those in their forties. The number of self-employed in the forty- to - forty four age range, which had been 1.2 million in 1991, had declined to less than half that, 500,000, in the year 2000.

Attention has focused on self-employment as a potential means of ensuring employment opportunities for older workers. But the key to a future increase in the number of older self-employed is to increase opportunities for self-employment while they are still young. If a person is unable to start a business and get it on track during his/her thirties or forties, self-employment at a later age will be difficult. It would require extraordinary ability, perseverance, and stamina for someone who had

**Fig. 8-2 Fluctuations in the Number of Self-Employed**
**(Non-farm and -forestry businesses; 10,000 people)**

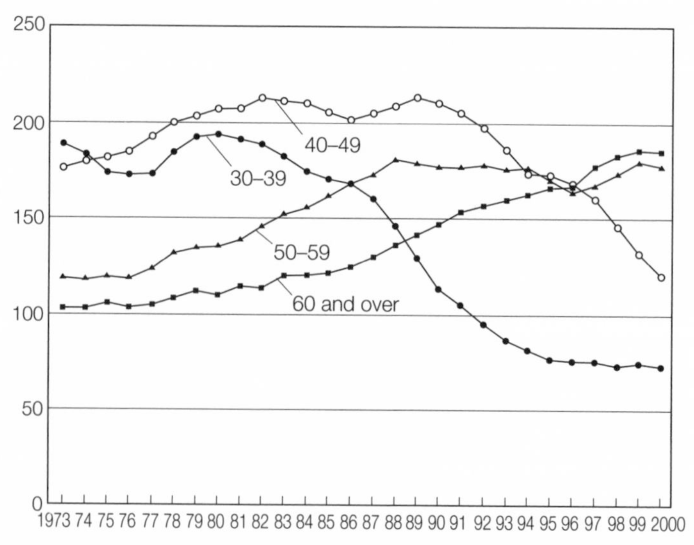


*Source*: Statistics Bureau, Management and Coordination Agency, *Labour Force Survey*

been a salaried worker until his/her early fifties to then go into business for him/herself and make a success of it. In that sense, the decline in self-employment that is occurring today among those in their thirties and forties portends a decline in employment opportunities for tomorrow's seniors.

As one ages, two mutually contradictory tendencies are involved in the choice of self-employment. The first is that advancing age is likely to encourage self-employment. The knowledge and experience a person has accumulated over the years can help him/her avoid the uncertainties involved in self-employment and acquire the means to overcome the difficulties that the work entails. On the other hand, advancing age is also likely to discourage self-employment. If, after years of continuous service, a salaried employee is promoted to a management or an executive position, that may satisfy the desire for independence, and he/she may cease to think about opening a business, with all the risks that go along with it. As one's stamina declines and the need increases for a steady income to buy a home or educate one's children, the willingness to take a chance and opt for self-employment also declines.

The number of people who opt to become self-employed in their thirties and forties when they are at their prime has been drastically declining in Japan. The tendency that discourages the choice of self-employment outweighs the one that encourages it, and for many people there has been a growing trend to avoid self-employment, where business uncertainties loom so large. (For further details, see Genda Yūji and Kambayashi Ryō, "Declining Self-employment in Japan" *Journal of the Japanese and International Economies*, 16, (2002) 73–91.

In addition, as we saw in the preceding chapter, forming a wide-ranging human network that extends beyond one's workplace or family circle is a significant factor for those who are independence oriented. Active participation in the community outside the workplace is important if one wants to set up one's own business. But by the thirties and forties it becomes difficult to form new human relations. This is an impediment to a potential future job change or business startup. A wide circle of relationships is necessary to transform the nagging uncertainties that surround job change or self-employment into risks that can be coolly challenged.

## Global trends

Throughout the economic slowdown of the 1990s, attention focused on restructuring and the rising pressure to make staff reductions resulting from it. But the number of employees (those working for wages) did not, in fact, go down; it went up during the 1990s by more than five million, from 48.35 million in 1990 to 53.56 million in 2000, according to the *Labour Force Survey*. Even after the bubble economy collapsed in 1992, the workforce increased by more than two million. By contrast, the number of self-employed and family employees has drastically declined, by more than a million each. The reason the total number of workers has hardly risen at all since the bubble burst has nothing to do with employees experiencing restructuring. It is due to the decline in the number of self-employed and family employees.

Very small self-employed businesses compare unfavorably to large companies when it comes to productivity. Is it natural, then, that they should decline as an economy matures? Figure 8-3 compares fluctuations in the number of self-employed in industrialized countries. Far from declining, in most countries the number went up not just in the 1990s but even in the medium to long term during the 1980s and 1990s. Great Britain in the 1980s and the Netherlands and Germany in the 1990s experienced a steep rise in self-employment. Only a few countries saw self-employment decline in both the short term and the medium to long term: Denmark, France, and Japan.

When those who opted for self-employment are asked their reasons for doing so, in every country, "I want to be my own boss" invariably tops the list. According to the OECD *Employment Outlook* for 1992 (page 170), the desire "to be one's own boss" is cited as the most important reason for opening one's own business. Wanting to "be one's own boss" is important in Japan as well. But the desire to be independent has, on the whole, diminished here. Many Japanese are beginning to feel that they don't want to assume positions of responsibility.

The system of long-term employment found primarily at large companies has been regarded as an important reason why Japan's unemployment rate has traditionally been lower than in other industrialized countries. The strength of the "discouraged worker" effect among women has also been cited: when Japanese women lose their jobs, they tend not to join the ranks of the unemployed but give up looking for work altogether and become stay-at-home housewives or domestic helpers. But another reason is that, even in a recession, job opportunities have, to some extent, been guaranteed. Regardless of economic trends, there is usually a certain percentage of business startups, and, as these companies grow, they generate new employment opportunities.

In Japan, more people work at small and medium-sized companies than in other industrialized countries. That is how plentiful small and medium-sized companies are here. The reason for this is not simply that there are policies in place to protect them. Though some companies are driven into bankruptcy and forced to shut down, new microbusinesses as well as small and medium-sized ones have constantly come into existence and created employment opportunities. (For further details, see Teruyama Hiroshi and Genda Yūji, "Koyō Kikai no Sōshutsu to Sōshitsu no Henka—1986 kara 1998 no *Koyō Dōkō*

**Fig. 8-3 Average Annual Growth Rates of Self-Employment**
**(Excluding the agricultural sector)**

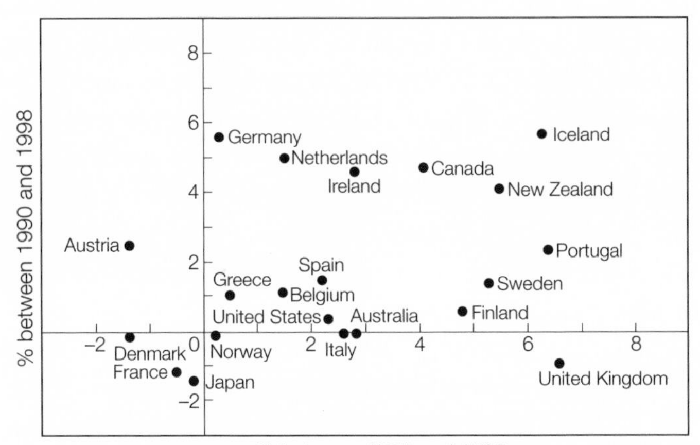


*Source*: OECD, *Employment Outlook* (2000), 159

*Chōsa* ni Motozuku Bunseki" [Fluctuations in the Creation and Destruction in Japan : Evidence from the Employment Trend Survey (1986–1998)], *Nihon Rōdō Kenkyū Zasshi* [Japanese Journal of Labour Studies], January 2002.)

The motivating force behind this job creation has been the steady emergence of small and medium-sized businesses, including self-employed ones. Their efficiency as a pump primer suddenly weakened in the late 1990s.

## Women should become their own bosses

Self-employment trends contain another shocking number as well. A glance at the OECD *Employment Outlook* for the year 2000 shows that the industrialized country which suffered the largest decline in the 1990s in self-employed businesses headed by women is, again, Japan. A closer look reveals that the direct cause, statistically speaking, is the precipitous drop in those doing piecework jobs at home that had been added by self-employment. Even more serious, however, is the fact that self-employment among women owner-managers who have taken on staff has barely risen at all since the 1980s when the economy was becoming more service oriented. In the 1990s, the decline in the category "self-employed with employees" is more conspicuous among women than among men.

Turning to trends for women in the labour market, women who are unemployed lose their incentive to work and drop out of the labour market; in short, they are counted as "not in the workforce." This tendency has been growing sharply in recent years (*White Paper on Labour* [2000], 36 and passim). It has been maliciously described as pseudo-unemployment only for the duration of the benefit period so that women who have no real desire to work can collect unemployment insurance. But that is probably not a real problem. Far more serious is the discouraged worker effect on unemployed women who give up searching for work altogether because, no matter how hard they look, there are no job opportunities that appeal to them.

An indescribable sense of paralysis and stagnation pervades Japanese society today. This mood will be dispelled when women, unable to display their real skills in business organizations, bid farewell to the male-dominated employment world and start their own companies *en masse.* The time has come for women to strike out on their own and grasp success in their own hands. The success they achieve may be the income they make, the pride they take in their work, or their sense of purpose and accomplishment. Japanese society will have taken a giant step forward toward becoming a society in which men and women enjoy an equal share in the planning when it is a realistic choice for women to be their own boss either as an owner-manager or in the professions, in sales or in a trade.

New types of self-employment are being devised that women have never engaged in before. New self-employed businesses, which make use of the franchise system and independent contracts, have been springing up one after another. The self-employment path is wide open not just for women but for others who feel a sense of job insecurity. It is both a key to economic revitalization and a safety net against job loss.

Japan will soon need to think seriously about policies that specifically target business startups by women and young people. A number of programs to promote self-employment especially among these two groups are already being established in Europe and North America (OECD, *Employment Outlook* [2000], 183–186 and passim). In addition, Japan needs support programs that concentrate on skill development so that high school graduates, who are steadily losing out on full-time job opportunities, can open their own businesses.

If I may speak bluntly, in most cases, the instant women quit their jobs and stay home, their personal network narrows. That is a problem. Even stay-at-home housewives form strong, close networks with their neighbors and other mothers. But the ability to survive the trials and tribulations of running a business does not depend on close relationships with people one sees all the time but rather on having an extensive network of friends whom one meets infrequently and with whom one can consult about any subject. Friends and acquaintances outside the workplace who can act as advisers are important for women who are independence oriented. For such women, relationships with people who are impartial but reliable, relationships that bind them to others by informal, wide-ranging but firm ties are indispensable.

Independence does not mean, however, that everything from start to finish has to be done by one person alone. Whether or not an independent or self-employed business successfully gets on track depends on the ability to build a good team of dependable collaborators who will provide the appropriate support. To do so, women must have begun long ago making a conscious effort to participate in the community outside their own family and workplace and to build a wide circle of friends with whom they are linked casually but firmly. Deep relationships with colleagues at work or with housewives in the neighborhood are all well and good, but a woman has a slim chance of opening a business or branching out on her own based on these alone.

Building informal, broadly based, yet firm human relationships also requires support from the social system. Community colleges and other such institutions, where a self-employed woman or; female owner-manager can enroll easily yet in all seriousness when she needs to know something about the law or business, ought to be more readily available outside the metropolitan areas. There is no guarantee that a creative owner-manager will have first-rate knowledge or expertise in personnel or labour management. A full range of placement services are needed so that middle-aged or older men with long experience in corporate personnel management could become important business partners at companies headed by women. This would provide new employment opportunities for older men, make use of their knowledge and experience, and give them a new work incentive.

From the perspective of society as a whole, it is also important to create an atmosphere in which women's attempts to open their own business or become self-employed are taken more seriously and are more positively appraised. Frankly speaking, the status quo for women is bleak. Female employees still find themselves in the unfortunate position of being forced to decide between work and family. Their situation has been slowly improving with the proliferation and improvement of day care and home care services. Most women who have chosen (or are considering choosing) to start their own business or become self-employed, however, still feel pressured to choose between work and family, and this is one of the reasons for a sense of impasse.

## The "right time" for a startup

Not just women but many freeters and young people feel they would like to be their own boss, and as a result, the number of independent startups is increasing. These will break down the existing roadblocks and offer a way out of the present impasse. Is it a good thing, then, if the number of school-aged CEOs and venture capitalists increases? Or does a startup begun by a middle-aged or older person with a certain amount of experience stand a better chance of being successful? In short, is there a "right time" to open an independent business? What sort of career does a person need to have had, when should the decision to start a business be made, and when should it be implemented for the highest likelihood of success? What kind of person is suited to be an entrepreneur? Let us analyze the statistical data and look at the profile that emerges of those who succeed.

People no doubt have different ideas about what constitutes success when it comes to opening a new business. Among those who have actually done so, a significantly high percentage feels that such things as job satisfaction and flexibility are important. "I want to work at my own pace," "I want to test my abilities," "I want to advance my career" always top the list of motives for starting one's own business. And yet, the fact is, even though the work itself may be enjoyable, it is hard to run a business without maintaining a certain level of earnings. From society's perspective, only a startup which is successful in the sense that it generates plenty of profits is worth supporting and cultivating. Let us listen to what the data can tell us about the sort of career an entrepreneur needs to have had for his/her business to be profitable and a source of high productivity.

Here I would like to look at the appropriate age and number of years of experience needed for a successful startup; for a more detailed discussion of the data and the analytical method, please refer to "The data speak" at the end of the chapter. How old does one need to be, and how many years of related job experience does one need to have, to maximize sales and earnings after opening a new business? In order to find this out, it is necessary to exclude the impact of other factors that affect earnings. These include the entrepreneur's gender, schooling, parents' occupation, size of the company at which he/she previously worked, amount of personal assets, type of occupation, membership in a franchise, and how long the business has existed. After eliminating the effects of these factors through regression analysis, it is possible to find the optimal number of years of experience and the optimal age for opening a new business from the standpoint of maximizing profits. The results are given in table 8-1.

In terms of maximizing both net profit (i.e., monthly revenues minus purchases) and income, the optimal age to open a new business is the late thirties to just over forty. The optimal number of years of related experience is 21.1 for net profit and 20.5 for income (for further details on the calculation method, see "The data speak" at the end of the chapter). The conclusions reached from these figures are very clear: if one is to make an economic success of a new business, it is most desirable to launch it when one is around forty after having accumulated the necessary know-how and expertise during twenty years or so of related work experience.

It turns out that there is a right time to open one's own business after all.

**Table 8-1 Optimal Number of Years of Experience/Age at Time of Startup/Personal Assets for Maximizing Profits**

| | Optimal age |
|---|---|
| Net profit<br>Income | 40.5<br>37.3 |
| | Optimal number of years' experience |
| Net profit<br>Income | 21.1<br>20.5 |
| | Optimal amount of assets (million yen) |
| Net profit<br>Income | 36.932<br>40.493 |

*Source*: Genda Yūji, "Kaigyō no Shun" (The Right Time for a Startup) (discussion paper, Institute of Social Science, University of Tokyo, Tokyo, September 2001.)

Along with the optimal age and number of years of experience, it is also possible to calculate the optimal level of personal financial assets. A glance at table 8-1 shows that the figures are extremely high, 36.932 million yen to maximize net profit and 40.493 million to maximize earnings and income. Considering that average personal assets for 1998 was 4.778 million, the optimal level is extremely high. That does not mean, however, that an entrepreneur who does not have in excess of 40 million yen worth of personal assets cannot succeed economically. It simply means that any amount over that figure has no effect on success or failure, but, under (ordinary) circumstances, when someone has less than 40 million yen, the more assets has, the higher the earnings one is likely to make. Generally speaking, the more personal assets one has, the more likely one is to succeed economically. That is only natural.

If one has related job experience and can supply one's own personal assets, is it more beneficial to have worked for a large company or a small to medium-sized one? From the results in "The data speak" at the end of the chapter, we see that working for a small or medium-sized firm is more advantageous than working for a large one. Post-startup net profit was clearly greater for those who had worked for a company with more than five but fewer than 300 employees prior to opening their own businesses. Experience working at a firm with a staff of from five to nineteen people or from twenty to forty-nine people is also linked to an increase in income. By contrast, prior experience at a large company with either 300 to 999 or more than 1,000 employees is not related to an increase in profits. Presumably, it is easier to acquire the knowledge and expertise needed to run a business at a small or medium-sized firm than at a large company.

The reason a startup business makes a profit has nothing to do with work experience at a big company, educational achievement, or even one's parent's occupation. Rather, it involves making it a specific goal, right after graduation, to go into business for one's self at around age forty and, for the next twenty years or so, steadily acquiring related work experience at a small or medium-sized company.

## Getting through hard times

We learned from the preceding discussion that it is desirable for the owner of a startup business to be around forty years of age and have around twenty years of related work experience since graduation. Has there been a steady rise in self-employment among forty-year-olds to reflect these favorable conditions? As figure 8-2 shows, the truth is the exact opposite.

Why have independent startups been declining among those in their forties despite the fact that forty ought to be an economically advantageous age to open a new business? Although it may be favorable to start a company at age forty, income thereafter drops significantly. Using the Management and Coordination Agency's *National Survey on Family Income and Expenditures,* figure 8-4 looks at the relationship between age and business income for the self-employed in non-farm and -forestry businesses who reside in the Tokyo, Nagoya, and Osaka metropolitan areas. Self-employed business income for those in their late thirties and forties rose little if at all between 1989 and 1994; if anything, it went down.

There are any number of reasons why self-employed income might decline for those in their prime. Computerization and the emerging service economy work to the advantage of those who are younger and better able than those in their forties to deal with such changes. The intense competition generated by the Large-Scale Retail Store Law and

**Fig. 8-4 Relation between Age and Income of Self-Employed**
**(In non-farm and -forestry businesses who reside in the Tokyo, Osaka, and Nagoya metropolitan areas)**

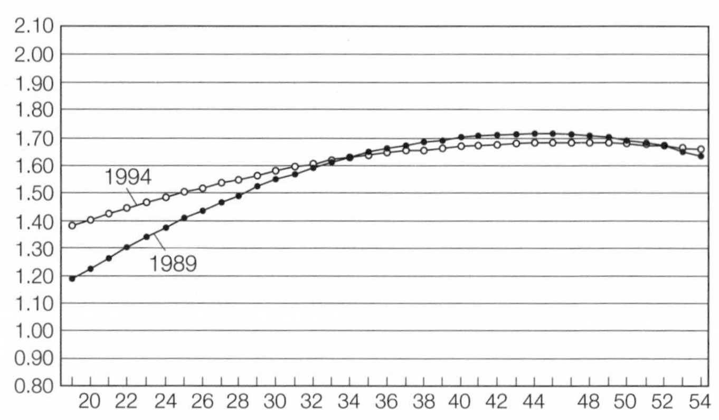


*Source*: Genda Yūji and Kambayashi Ryō, "Declining Self-Employment in Japan," *Journal of the Japanese and International Economies* 16 (March 2002): 73–91
*Note*: All incomes are natural logarithms. Differences in income by age are expressed in terms of the percent by which incomes differ.

other forms of deregulation worked to the disadvantage of the existing self-employed who were approaching middle or old age. The collapse of the bubble economy lowered the self-employment income of middle-aged and older workers who had opened their businesses before the bubble burst. The list goes on and on; in short, many conditions exist that have been unfavorable to middle-aged and older self-employed. In any event, despite the fact that forty is the ideal age to open one's own business, the earnings environment at the beginning of the 1990s was undoubtedly severe.

In addition, making it through the harsh business conditions of the very first year or two is particularly difficult for independent startups. Figure 8-5 shows the relationship between monthly earnings of all kinds and the number of months that have elapsed since the business opened. The figures here are the median earnings for each month since startup. If monthly averages were used, the results would be greatly skewed by occasional favorable earnings; thus, the focus here has been on the median (the exact midway point). Not only does the earnings environment not improve right after startup, monthly revenues continue to worsen until the first year and a half. Although net profit gradually

**Fig. 8-5 Relation between Number of Years since Opening and (Median) Monthly Profit**

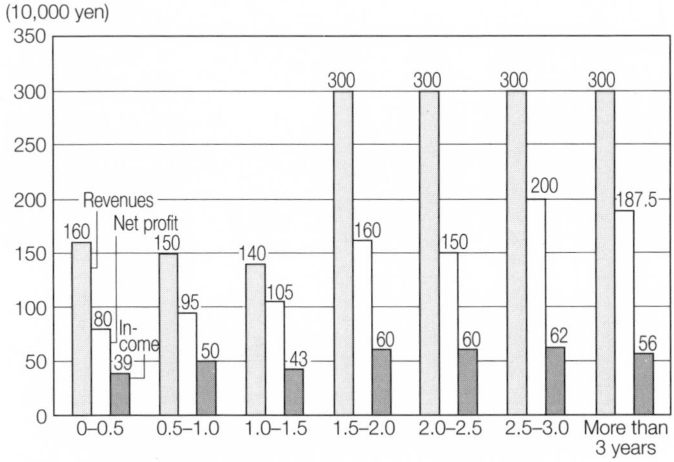

*Source*: Genda Yūji, "Kaigyō no Shun" (The Right Time for a Startup) (discussion papers, Institute of Social Science, University of Tokyo, Tokyo, September 2001)

increases, income hardly goes up at all. For that reason, some entrepreneurs are forced to give up during this period.

If they make it through the first two years, however, the business environment takes a turn for the better. Monthly revenues hold steady at around the three million yen level, and net profit doubles to nearly two million yen. Monthly income, too, rises to around 600,000 yen. The touchstone is around two years after opening. The decline among self-employed in their forties during the 1990s is a sign that it is becoming quite difficult for forty-year-olds, who theoretically ought to be just the right age to start a business, to make it through the tough business environment during the first year or two. Figure 8-6 shows the median profit and number of months since opening for entrepreneurs between the ages of thirty-five and forty-four. Here, too, the harshness of the environment in those first two years is quite evident. Monthly revenues go down from two million yen right after opening to 1.5 million a year and a half later. Income, too, is about 400,000 yen, which is less than an employed worker of the same age would make. Even if earnings were

**Fig. 8-6 Number of Years since Opening and (Median) Monthly Profit in the Case of a Startup at Age 35–44**

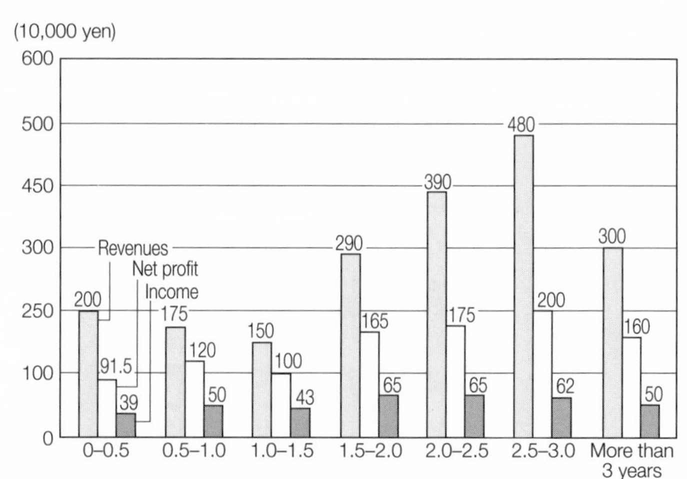


*Source*: Genda Yūji, "Kaigyō no Shun" (The Right Time for a Startup) (discussion paper, Institute of Social Science, University of Tokyo, Tokyo, September 2001)

higher, considering the sheer demands of the work involved, it would not be at all surprising if an owner-manager were to decide that owning one's own business was not worth the effort.

If he/she does not give up, however, but makes it through the second year, independence is by no means a bad choice. Once past the 2.5- to -3-year point, monthly revenues rise to 4.8 million yen. Net profit, which had been around a million yen during the first year to year and a half, doubles to two million. After the second year, income is stable at around 600,000 yen.

A business started at age forty has the potential to make a profit, but in order for it to actually do so, it needs support during the first few years. Without such assistance, it will be impossible to take advantage of the benefits of starting a business at forty.

## "Establishing one's stand" at forty

Confucius once said, "At fifteen, I aspired to learning. At thirty, I established my stand. At forty, I had no delusions. At fifty, I knew my destiny. At sixty, I knew the truth in all I heard. At seventy, I could follow the wishes of my heart without doing wrong." In terms of starting one's own business in Japan today, the time to "establish one's stand" is forty rather than thirty. (On the whole, this saying from the *Analects* would be more reflective of present realities if ten years were added to each age.) According to the data, forty is the optimal age for starting a business; startups opened just before or after that age have the highest likelihood of generating future profits. But, of course, that does not mean that a forty-year-old should impulsively go into business for him / herself. Success is unlikely for someone who has passed aimlessly through his/her twenties and thirties, then suddenly at forty comes up with the idea of starting a business. Rather, if a startup is to be an economic success, one needs to make plans for it right after graduation, then accumulate around twenty years of work experience in a related area. Related work experience is more conducive to future profitability if it is acquired at a small or medium-sized firm rather than at a large one. An owner-manager's academic background and his/her parent's occupation have no bearing on a startup's economic success.

A self-employed business that someone has started at around age forty after accumulating about twenty years of related work experience is a source of new net profit. At one time, we used to hear the expression *datsusara*, which might be translated "ex-salaried worker." The term came into vogue in the 1970s, when it was extremely unusual for middle-aged and older employees to quit their jobs and go into business for themselves. Today the situation remains basically unchanged; being a self-employed ex-employee is still unusual. Business startups by forty-year-olds need to become more commonplace; new microbusinesses with the potential for economic success need to spring up in great numbers. The reality is grim, however. Although forty ought to be an advantageous age to start a new business, the number of self-employed forty-year-olds in non-farm and -forestry areas dramatically declined in the 1990s. For middle-aged and older self-employed, the competition became tougher, and their earnings did not go up. They were unable to survive the tough business environment right after opening their businesses.

We are beginning to catch sight of ways to provide support to startups that have a good basis for growth. First, make it a clear social goal to support startup businesses by those who are around forty. Such companies will not only be a source of profit, they will also serve as a safety net at a time when society is aging and the unemployment rate is high. An environment in which even the unemployed, if they wish, can support themselves through self-employment is also related to ensuring a steady supply of employment opportunities. But if older workers are to have job opportunities as self-employed, it is too late for them to begin after they reach old age. Rather, they need to be encouraged to start their own businesses at around forty when they are in their prime.

Given the importance of having several years of experience, potential startup candidates will need to be cultivated from their twenties on. Young people must be encouraged, as early as possible, to begin formulating a long-term vision for opening their own business.

Support for the startup process may be important, but considering that the first one or two years after opening are the most difficult from a business perspective, support to help owner-managers get through those critical first years is even more important. Even though forty is supposed to be the right age for a startup, earnings for self-employed forty-year-olds are deteriorating. The most effective way to cultivate timely independent startups is to provide owner-managers with the support they need to weather the hard times right after opening.

A few years ago the world went through a tamagotchi boom. But the boom spontaneously ended as soon as these toys became readily available. The reason the startup boom and the venture boom of the 1990s have lasted so long is just the other way around: they have failed to find general acceptance. It is an undeniable fact that those who are already self-employed are having a hard time achieving either job satisfaction or adequate income. What Japan needs is a new breed of casual self-employed—perhaps we might call them the "new indies"—to emerge in great numbers among freeters. This will undoubtedly usher in a new economic phase. One of the concerns raised by the freeter question is skill development among young people; if they don't become full-time employees, they have no option but to do it themselves. Once the idea of becoming their own boss takes root, young workers will begin to confront the issue of skill development on their own. The reason full-time employment seems unattractive is that it is regarded as a dead end. If it is seen, instead, as a stepping-stone to becoming one's own boss, young people's views about becoming a full-time employee will surely change.

The future of the youth employment problem depends on whether or not young people decide they want to become their own boss.

**The data speak**

## The career needed for a successful startup

The sections entitled "The 'right time' for a startup" and "Getting through hard times" are the results of an analysis based on the *Survey of Actual Conditions at New Startups* (August 1998) conducted by the National Life Finance Corporation (NLFC). The survey that year was made of 6,648 companies that received financing from the NLFC between April and August 1997 and, at the time of financing, had been in business for less than a year (including some financed prior to opening); valid responses were received from 1,641 companies (for a valid response rate of 24.7 percent). The results, excluding companies whose type of business involved real estate and rental services, are given below.

The survey examined income in terms of (1) monthly revenues (an average of 4.226 million yen) and the following itemized expenditures:

(2) purchases (2.455 million yen),

(3) wages for the company representative and family members (431,000 yen),

(4) personnel expenses (in addition to [3], 665,000 yen),

(5) other expenditures (642,000 yen), and

(6) loan repayments (principal and interest, 224,000 yen).

The amount obtained by adding together (2) through (6) and subtracting the total from monthly reverues (1) is indicated as (7) income (249,000 yen).

What attracts our attention about the income and expenditure situation of a startup is, first, monthly revenues, second, the "net" amount when purchases are subtracted from monthly revenues, and, finally, profits, defined as the amount obtained by adding income to wages for the company representative and his/her family members. This amount (a natural logarithm) is regarded as an independent variable, and a regression analysis is performed.

When this is done, the factors observed as explanatory variables include not only the gender and number of years of schooling of the startup owner, but such things as the occupation of his/her parents at the time the decision to start a business was made; number of employees at the company where he/she previously worked; personal assets at the time of setting up the business (savings, separation pay, etc.) and its value squared and divided by 10,000; number of years of previous related work experience and its value squared and divided by 100; age at the time of opening and its value squared and divided by 100; number of months since opening; type of occupation (excluding real estate and rental services); and membership in a franchise. The reason squaring was added to several of these variables is that their estimated results were used to find the optimal values that would maximize profits after startup in these areas: amount of personal assets, number of years of related work experience, and age at which to open a business.

The method for calculating these optimal values is extremely simple. Let maximized earnings (either monthly revenues or net profit or income) be V, number of years of experience (or age at the time of startup) be X, and primary and secondary coefficients be a and b respectively; then, $X^*$, the optimal number of years of experience (or age at the time of startup) that maximizes the natural logarithm V, is found by the following equation

$$\frac{\Delta \ln V}{\Delta X} = a + \frac{2bX^*}{100} = 0 \Rightarrow X^* = \frac{100a}{-2b}$$

The results when regression analysis is performed are given in table 8-2. For both years of experience and age at the time of startup, the primary coefficients are positive, and the secondary coefficients are negative. The coefficients in almost all cases are statistically significant (have one or more asterisks). That means that, as long as other conditions are regarded as constant, there is an optimal number of years of experience at which monthly revenues, net profit, and income after opening, respectively, are maximized.

Using this method, the results of finding the optimal number of years of experience and the optimal age at time of startup are given in table 8-1. (It might be noted in passing that the method for calculating the

## Table 8-2 Factors That Enable Startups to Succeed Economically: Results of Regression Analysis

| | Profit (natural logarithm) | Monthly revenue | | Net profit | |
|---|---|---|---|---|---|
| | Explanatory variables | Coefficient | t-value | Coefficient | t-value |
| Gender <female> | Dummy for male | 0.3574 | 3.90*** | 0.3535 | 3.77*** |
| Academic attainment | Number of years of schooling | 0.0355 | 2.40*** | 0.0234 | 1.58 |
| Parents' occupation <government employee> | Employee | −0.0199 | −0.21 | −0.1061 | −1.14 |
| | Self-employed | −0.0178 | −0.19 | −0.0391 | −0.41 |
| | Farm or forestry worker | −0.1308 | −1.07 | −0.1352 | −1.08 |
| | Other | 0.0809 | 0.59 | −0.0023 | −0.02 |
| Previous company size <fewer than 4, including employees> | 5–19 | 0.2065 | 2.14** | 0.1851 | 1.91* |
| | 20–49 | 0.3263 | 2.94*** | 0.3657 | 3.30*** |
| | 50–99 | 0.2627 | 1.99** | 0.3050 | 2.34** |
| | 100–299 | 0.1881 | 1.49 | 0.3164 | 2.50** |
| | 300–999 | −0.0551 | −0.39 | −0.0118 | −0.08 |
| | 1,000 and over | −0.1427 | −1.07 | −0.0170 | −0.12 |
| | Other than employees | −0.0893 | −0.71 | 0.0193 | 0.15 |
| Personal assets | Personal assets | 0.0008 | 7.55*** | 0.0006 | 6.53*** |
| | Personal assets squared/10,000 | −0.0009 | −3.22*** | −0.0009 | −3.33*** |
| Number of years of experience | Number of years of related work experience | 0.0295 | 3.15*** | 0.0268 | 2.86*** |
| | Number of years of experience squared/100 | -0.0438 | −1.42 | −0.0636 | −2.04** |
| Age at time of startup | Age at time of startup | 0.0658 | 2.63*** | 0.0441 | 1.70* |
| | Age at time of startup squared/100 | −0.0801 | −2.69*** | −0.0545 | −1.75* |
| Number of months since opening | Number of months since opening | 0.0209 | 5.47*** | 0.0186 | 4.85*** |
| Type of occupation <dummy for transportation business, including taxi owners> | Manufacturing | 1.0767 | 5.52*** | 0.7198 | 3.46*** |
| | Wholesale | 1.7107 | 9.70*** | 0.6771 | 3.47*** |
| | Retail | 1.3491 | 8.14*** | 0.6439 | 3.46*** |
| | Restaurant | 0.7390 | 4.45*** | 0.4215 | 2.27** |
| | Personal services | 0.3470 | 2.09** | 0.3083 | 1.66* |
| | Business services | 0.9814 | 5.87** | 0.7610 | 4.07*** |
| | Construction | 1.4541 | 8.39*** | 1.0044 | 5.20*** |
| | Other | 0.7168 | 3.18** | 0.4277 | 1.68 |
| Franchise | Dummy for franchise membership | 0.3100 | 2.84*** | 1.2071 | 1.09 |
| | Constant | 1.2653 | 2.18** | 1.9766 | 3.28*** |
| | Sample size | 1.179 | | 958 | |
| | F-value | 24.24 | | 10.99 | |
| | Adjusted $R^2$ | 0. 3640 | | 0.2323 | |

*Note*: The greater the number of asterisks, the higher the statistical reliability of the results. A single asterisk indicates a 10% level of statistical reliability; two asterisks, a 5% level; and three asterisks, a 1% level. An item in angle brackets signifies a reference group for an explanatory variable. The number of years of schooling for those with advanced degrees is considered to be 18.

| Income | |
|---|---|
| Coefficient | t-value |
| 0.3347 | 3.37*** |
| 0.0094 | 0.60 |
| −0.1507 | −1.55 |
| −0.1406 | −1.41 |
| −0.2065 | −1.56 |
| 0.2066 | 0.18 |
| 0.2134 | 2.09** |
| 0.2497 | 2.13** |
| 0.1410 | 1.03 |
| 0.2201 | 1.64 |
| 0.0521 | 0.35 |
| 0.0289 | 0.20 |
| −0.1207 | −0.89 |
| 0.0004 | 4.19*** |
| −0.0005 | −1.97** |
| 0.0316 | 3.10*** |
| −0.0772 | −2.26** |
| 0.0494 | 1.79* |
| −0.0664 | −2.00** |
| 0.0127 | 3.14*** |
| 0.6261 | 2.89*** |
| 0.8583 | 4.23*** |
| 0.4403 | 2.28** |
| 0.0963 | 0.50 |
| 0.2052 | 1.07 |
| 0.6430 | 3.33*** |
| 0.8173 | 4.09*** |
| 0.4657 | 1.75* |
| 0.1264 | 1.05 |
| 1.5854 | 2.48** |
| 904 | |
| 8.67 | |
| 0.1976 | |

optimal amount of personal assets is basically the same as the equation above. The only difference is that the denominator for the second item on the right-hand side of the equation is 1,000 instead of 100.) For net profit, for example, since the coefficient for age at the time of opening and its value squared are a = 0.0441 and b = −0.0545,

$$(100 \times 0.0441) / (-2 \times -0.0545) = 40.46$$

From this it is determined that in order to maximize net profit, the optimal age at time of startup is around 40.5.

Using the same method, the optimal number of years of related work experience is calculated as 21.1 for net profit and 20.5 for income.

A glance at table 8-2 shows that some of the coefficients for previous company size are positive numbers with asterisks. The experience of having worked for a small company is more conducive to profit than having worked for a large company.

In addition, the coefficients for all the independent variables under "Number of months since opening" are positive and statistically significant (in the case of net profit, it is 0.0186 with three asterisks). The more time that has elapsed since opening, the greater the improvement in profits. To put it another way, this means that the period immediately after opening is tough not only for monthly revenues but also for net profit and income. In terms of a startup policy, support for startups in the period right after opening is more effective than support to get the business started in the first place.

Turning to types of occupation, earning conditions are worse for personal services businesses (services businesses whose main customers are ordinary consumers) than for manufacturing and construction. Personal services businesses are not statistically significant for either income or profit. Although personal services such as child care and home care are expected to grow, conditions for startups in these areas, in fact, continue to be bleak

It is also true that startups headed by women do not generate as much earnings as those headed by men. It may be that women have a stronger tendency than men to put the nature of the work ahead of profits. Even so, it will be an important task to improve the earnings environment for independent businesses headed by women as a way of making self-employment a promising option for diversifying job opportunities for women.

A more detailed account of the above is found in "*Shinki Kaigyō Jittai Chōsa* no Saibunseki" (A Re-analysis of the Recent *Survey of Actual Conditions at New Startups*) (September 2001) in the SSJ Data Archive Research Paper Series, Institute of Social Science, University of Tokyo.

# *Conclusion*

# ***Talking to Seventeen-year-olds***

## Why aren't there any jobs?

Many grown-ups complain about today's young people. "Their attitude toward work has gotten soft," they say. "They can't stick at anything." "They quit at the slightest criticism." Lots of adults are worried that young high school graduates who don't go on to college won't get full-time jobs but become freeters or take part-time jobs instead. I don't for a minute believe there's been a sudden decline recently in young people's attitudes toward work. Students in my day used to be called *shinjinrui*—the "new human species"—a term that's now utterly obsolete. I bet that the older generation who called us that were the target of complaints about "today's young people" when they were young.

Grown-ups are free to grumble all they like that today's young people are no good. But when the government starts saying it, that's an entirely different matter. The government is beginning to think seriously that it needs to implant a greater sense of job consciousness in young people in order to stop the spread of freeters. Plans to make community service compulsory at schools and to give young people firsthand experience of working life through internships are intended to instill job consciousness. That would be OK, I suppose, if it succeeded in giving everyone a sense of how really interesting work can be. But that's probably expecting too much. First of all, there's something a bit off-putting about the idea that any teenager might feel work is interesting after a few days, or at most a few weeks, of being an intern.

There's a proverb in Japanese about "growing up watching the boss's back." The true meaning of jobs and work is something that's acquired over time by making mistakes and being severely tested. In the past, most businesses and workshops were in the home so, in the natural course of things, it was possible to get a sense of how hard work really is. In times like today, though, when most adults prefer to work in offices, most kids have never seen the sort of work their parents do. That's why it's only natural that they don't have any real sense of what it means to work.

It's asking too much to eliminate freeters and change attitudes toward work. The reason for the rise in the number of freeters and the increase in job flipping among young people may, in part, be a matter of attitudes, but the real reason is the recession. Even high school students know that in a recession there are no jobs. But the lack of full-time jobs is not due just to the recession alone. There was an issue of *Playboy Weekly* a while ago on why freeters are increasing that I expect some of you may have seen. When I read it, my reaction was this: "You claim that the reason freeters are on the rise is due to a weak sense of job consciousness among young people, but there are structural problems in society that predate this. Simply put, there's not much doubt that jobs for young people are being slashed as a way of protecting the jobs of middle-aged and older workers. The first step is to solve that problem. No good will come from picking on the younger generation alone." That's putting it a bit strongly, I suppose. But that's what I'd like to say.

To compensate for protecting the jobs of middle-aged and older workers, employment opportunities for young people are declining. There's been a lot of talk about restructuring, but, in fact, hardly any middle-aged and older college graduates have lost their jobs. Large companies that employ lots of college grads are, for all intents and purposes, unable to let workers go. If a company is taken to court on a charge of unfair dismissal, most courts will decide against the company. That's why companies can't dismiss their middle-aged and older workers even though they're overstaffed. And so, they adjust for overstaffing by not hiring any young people.

This surplus situation will continue until at least 2010 or thereabouts, when the huge baby boom generation finally retires. Right now, retirement is generally at sixty, but there's a move to amend the law and extend the mandatory retirement age to sixty-five so that older workers can work longer. If that happens, the trend for middle-aged and older workers to steal jobs away from young people will get even stronger. They parcel out all the physically demanding work to the young, and all the jobs worth doing they monopolize for themselves and don't pass them on to young people. What's more, in a recession, it becomes harder and harder to find a workplace that's really appealing, that provides a sense of accomplishment in one's work. That's why young people don't become full-time employees; that's why they change jobs. It has nothing to do with a weakening work ethic. Let me put it to you bluntly. The reason there aren't any good jobs for you is the grown-ups' fault.

## And yet . . .

OK, let's assume grown-ups are to blame, society's to blame; then what? Is there no way out? Even among freeters, some take a hard look at the grim realities and behave coolly, others do not. Some freeters who take being a freeter seriously say they don't want to have anything to do with other freeters. So, even though they may all be called freeters, there are many differences in attitudes and ways of thinking among them. That's why I cannot and will not say that you should never under any circumstances become a freeter or that freeters ought to behave in such-and-such a way.

Still, what all freeters can be said to have in common is this: in the long run, they have to protect themselves, and they have to do it by themselves. If you are a full-time employee in a company, there's someone in the company in charge of things like salary and pension who takes care of everything for you without your having to do a thing about it. But that's not the way it works in the case of freeters. They have to do everything for themselves. Sometimes, because they don't have the information or the know-how, they may be cheated by their employer and end up being overworked. Unlike full-time employees, freeters are easy to cheat in many ways, and they often get taken advantage of. For example, many of you, I expect, have part-time jobs; when you started working, did you receive a document in which things like your wages and days off were written down? A company by law must always provide such a document. If you didn't get one, you have no proof if the company doesn't pay you the salary it promised or makes you work longer hours than you agreed to. You'll inevitably be forced into an unfavorable position.

It really all depends on how freeters handle the matter. The best thing is for them to know in advance how to protect themselves.

## Don't "try hard" at your job

What, then, is the most useful thing that a freeter or a full-time employee should know about working? I'd like to talk now about a way of thinking that, on the emotional side, may be beneficial to have. I'm not saying, though, that this is what you have to do. Rather, I'm saying that you'd be better off if you didn't do this, or it's all right not to do it. After all, not doing something's a lot easier than doing something, isn't it?

The first thing you'd be better off not doing is *this*: try to avoid the casual use of the expression *gambaru*, "I will try hard," at work. Or suppose, for example, not necessarily you, but a friend of yours, gets a job somewhere, then gets upset and worried because the work is too hard and doesn't know whether to quit or not. It would be better not to automatically tell him/her to *gambare*, "hang in there," without really thinking about it. Psychiatrists and counselors never tell neurotic patients to "try hard." And they advise their patients' families never to use that expression either. Do you know why? Because most people suffering from neuroses try too hard to begin with. Telling a person like that to try hard or try harder will only make them feel even more trapped than they do already.

There's been a tremendous surge in the percentage of adult who, when asked how they would describe how they feel about the world, respond "unhappy." The feeling is slowly taking hold among grown-ups that nothing comes of trying hard, that it doesn't matter if you try hard or not. That's something teenagers probably understand instinctively.

Why, then, do I make it a point of saying, "Don't say *gambaru*"? Because Japanese has no other term of encouragement except that word. If you watch the sports news on television, almost every interviewer says *gambatte kudasai,* and almost every athlete promises to do so. What, precisely, are they telling them to do? I once saw a TV documentary on Takahashi Naoko, who won a gold medal in the women's marathon at the Sydney Olympics. The program on NHK covered the 42.195 kilometers up until she won the medal. Prior to the race, Takahashi had trained hard in the expectation that her main rival would be the world record holder, Tegla Loroupe of Kenya. "I won't win a gold if I don't beat Loroupe," she told herself. As it turned out, during the race, Loroupe was never once in contention and didn't win a medal. Until the middle of the race, though, everyone in contention including Takahashi kept worrying about when Loroupe was going to catch up to them. Around the twenty-second kilometer, Takahashi decided to make her move. The advice her coach Koide Yoshio gave her at that moment wasn't "*Gambare,* Takahashi!" He kept saying over and over, "Loroupe isn't coming." At the most critical point midway through the race, what advice or encouragement did Takahashi need most? In that tense moment, probably nothing could have been simpler or more to the point than "Loroupe isn't coming." With truly perfect timing, her coach gave Takahashi the most useful words of encouragement he could possibly have given her. And when she heard those words, Takahashi was able to coolly calculate that all she needed to do to win a gold was to beat Lidia Simon of Romania, who was running alongside of her. The result, as you all know, was that Takahashi became the first Japanese woman to win an Olympic gold medal in a track-and-field event.

That's why I don't plan to tell you, "No matter how tough things may be, keep on working hard." There's no point saying something like that. I have no intention whatsoever to stand here on this platform and tell all of you collectively to try hard. If I thought seriously about what I wanted to say to you, what words of encouragement to give you, it probably wouldn't do any good unless I got down off this platform and spent a lot of time listening individually to what each and every one of you had to say. How else could I possibly say anything that would be just right for each of you? Whether I could do that or not would be a test of my own seriousness.

At any rate, try not to say, "I will try hard" without thinking deeply about the work you are doing. Stop saying, "try hard" when you are sincerely trying to encourage someone else. That means you need to take a much closer look at that person. The important thing is to find your own words of encouragement that will help him/her to fight coolly. When you're working, don't say to yourself, "I will try hard to do *x*," instead, try to think the situation through and tell yourself, "in order to make *x* happen, I need to do *y*." Surprisingly, the way will open up from that point on.

## What, then, should you "do"?

You might think, then, that it would be OK if you didn't simply try hard, but just did the best you could, but that's really difficult. As I said at the beginning, people who bumble along being freeters often get cheated, taken advantage of, and end up being overworked. Even though you stop aimlessly trying hard, it is important, I think, to have some clear desires of your own.

Grown-ups often tell young people like you to "have a dream." But I'd like to tell you that it's OK if you don't. It's better not to have a dream, if that's all you have. Successful artists and CEOs don't have dreams; they are already taking specific steps to make their dreams come true. Someone who says, "My dream is to become an actress" is never going to become an actress. Only a person who auditions unsuccessfully time and time again yet never loses her desire to be an actress will ever become one. On the radio the other day, a listener asked Yamashita Tatsurō, "Was it your dream when you were young to become a successful singer?" "I was too bound up in my music to have any time for dreams," Yamashita replied. That's probably the way most truly successful people feel.

I certainly think it's important to have dreams. But too often people have dreams but never do anything about them because they think it will be too hard. They may, of course, have dreams in order to escape the harshness of reality, but that's not going to make reality the slightest bit easier. Instead of having a dream, it's more important to have the clear intention of becoming your own boss.

My job is to teach economics and to think about economics. People tend to think that economics is the study of how to make money. In fact, though, economics is about thinking what all of us who live in society need to do to make our lives a bit happier than they are now. There's a secret to living a happy life. The secret that economics teaches is surprisingly simple: "You can be happy if you do the opposite of what everyone else is doing. If you have 'scarcity value,' you will be rated highly." In Japan, the number of people who want to be their own boss is declining. According to that questionnaire survey I just mentioned, most grown-ups think the world is an unhappy place; an increasing number also say that they don't want to assume positions of responsibility. They don't want to become a boss with lots of responsibility but would rather follow comfortably behind someone else. Since no one wants to be one, becoming a boss has scarcity value. The likelihood of happiness is high.

Of course, there are a lot of different ways of being a boss. Probably the first thing that comes to mind is the head of a company or a CEO. But people who run their own businesses, in other words, the self-employed, are also bosses, and they have been dropping out in droves. In fact, France and Japan are the only industrialized countries where the self-employment rate outside the agricultural sector keeps going down. Japan's weak point today is that if you ask people, "Who wants to be their own boss?" very few raise their hands. Those who go to first-rate universities, especially, want to work for as long as possible at a large company and draw a steady salary. They don't think about becoming a boss where the risk of failure is great.

After you graduate from high school and become a freeter, little by little acquire the know-how to run a store. Learn how to get part-time workers to be enthusiastic about working for you. That way the number of freeters who become managers will slowly increase, and freeters will cease to be a problem. Quite the opposite; such freeters will be welcome.

When I talk about becoming your own boss, it may sound like I am speaking about men, but, in fact, women have a high likelihood of successfully becoming their own boss. In almost all the industrialized countries, the number of self-employed women rose during the 1990s; Japan was the only place where it went down. That's why self-employed women have real scarcity value. Women may think that it's hard to become the president of a company and impossible to balance it with a family and private life, but, surprisingly, that isn't so. A friend of mine who heads her own firm told me, "When all is said and done, I am most free being the head of my own company." That's certainly true. Nobody outranks you.

In any event, no matter what the circumstances may be, if you keep holding on to the feeling that you want to be your own boss, you will protect yourselves. And that, I believe, is what will lead you to have the power to make your dreams in the real sense come true.

## Having friends you can count on

It isn't actually easy, of course, to become your own boss. In fact, it's far more difficult right after startup. Above all, it's very lonely. You have to make all the final decisions by yourself. And, depending on the decisions you make, you may even fail. In these lonely circumstances, what you need in order to make the right decisions is to have pals you can rely on. The CEOs who set up Sony and Honda are well known, but they had friends who were no less admirable. You've heard the expression a "right-hand man"; a reliable pal who can tell you clearly that your judgment is mistaken is indispensable for a boss. How do you find such a pal? Among your friends. You probably all have close friends that you are constantly exchanging e-mail with. In the future, when something is bothering you, your family or your girlfriend or boyfriend will help you, but there will be times when the advice and encouragement of friends will be most welcome.

Friends are important. And yet, if possible, I hope you will make lots of friends not only with people you are in close and frequent contact with, but also with those you don't meet very often but, when you do, you can speak to directly from your heart. Close friends you see often, as a rule, will only tell you things you already know. That's because they're in the same boat you are. On the other hand, friends who live and work in a completely different environment than you do will often have completely different values and ways of thinking from you. You can receive unexpected hints from them, and they will give you new points of view when you need to take action of some kind. Of course, we are assuming that these people are friends you can really count on. Someday, when you are worrying about moving on to a new job or starting your own company, you will be more successful if you act on the advice of friends you meet infrequently. The data back this up.

Some of your high school friends you will hardly ever see again after graduation. But I hope that now, while you're still in school, you'll make lots of friends you can talk frankly to, even though you don't see each other very often. Why? So that someday you can successfully become your own boss.

## If you run into trouble at work

So far my talk today has been about what will be useful for you along the road that lies ahead. I guess I ought to say something a bit more specific about what you should do after graduation. Whether you're a full-time or a part-time employee, there are things you'll need to know about what to do if you run into problems at work. For example, if the salary is not what you were originally promised. If the company does a flit and you can't get paid. If you suddenly get fired even though you did nothing wrong. If you work dozens of hours a week with no time off. If you don't get paid for overtime. If you're injured on the job. If you're sexually harassed. There's no guarantee such things won't happen someday.

Just as you would go to the police if you ran into trouble in your everyday life, if you run into trouble at work, please go to the police that specialize in workers' problems: the Labour Standards Inspection Office. There are lots of branch offices near here in Mukōjima, Adachi, Edogawa, Ōji, Ikebukuro. You can find their addresses and telephone numbers on their website or in job information magazines like *From A*. If you go to a Labour Standards Inspection Office, they will give you specific advice on all sorts of topics. Even if you have been sexually harassed or treated unfairly at work, you can't protect your rights if you can't prove it. That's why they'll advise you to keep a diary and write down every single incident that happens at work.

It's often said that freeters have no security. But if you work more than thirty hours a week, it's the company's responsibility to pay the cost of insurance premiums. There are actually some companies that pretend not to know this, so when this happens, you would be wise to seek advice. The best thing is not to run into problems in your work. In fact, I personally have been lucky enough never to have had any problem that I needed to consult the Labour Standards Inspection Office about. But that's because universities are a sheltered sort of environment. Will all the workplaces that you will be working at be as protected as mine is? Frankly speaking, the answer is no. That's why you need to think ahead about how to prevent problems from happening. When you are looking for a job, choose a company that will clearly spell out the salary, the nature of the work, working hours, etc., and, if possible, will explain the conditions and the contents of the job not just orally but in a written document. Companies are required by law to do so. Please be aware that there's something suspicious about a company that dismisses a contract as a mere formality and doesn't give you precise explanations.

## What I really wanted to tell you

I meant to speak to you today about the road that lies ahead for high school students, but I may have gotten sidetracked. Still, I told you what I think you really ought to know about the reality behind the rising number of freeters.

You will be told to have a dream or to find work you really like, but, in fact, that's the hardest thing of all to do. And you'll worry because you don't find it.

In situations like these, I don't think grown-ups should simply tell freeters to become full-time employees and work hard at their jobs. Instead, I hope young people will have a strategy that is clearly all their own. That strategy is to have the feeling that, even if you don't have a dream, even if you don't find something you really want to do, somehow or other you will become your own boss. If you have a wide circle of friends you can count on, there's a chance that may happen. That's why I hope you'll make as many close friends as possible. If you do, I look forward to seeing a steady stream of people with a new and fascinating type of independent working style emerge from among you.

# *Epilogue*

The preceding chapter is a speech I planned to give to second-year students at a metropolitan Tokyo high school. I planned to, but never actually gave the speech. In fact, probably about half of what is written here I failed to deliver. Why? Because I got stage fright. Whether addressing academic conferences or international symposia, during the normal course of my teaching or when giving speeches I am occasionally asked to make, I have never ever tensed up and lost my composure (the one exception, which is invariably a disaster, is the speeches I am called on to give at wedding receptions). Not getting stage fright is probably not a good thing. On this particular day, however, I was extremely tense. To tell the truth, I started to get very nervous the day before.

The reason I happened to be talking to high school students in the first place was that a teacher at the school asked me to. We had written a high school textbook on contemporary society together. "At my high school it's time for a talk on life after graduation. Would you give it? You can talk about anything you like," he asked me, and I accepted.

When I mentioned to teachers at other high schools that I was going to speak at this particular school, quite frankly, they were surprised. The invariable response was a barrage of questions, "Really? You're going to speak at that school? Whatever for?" The school had a reputation of being a "problem school" with the lowest percentage of students going on to college of all the metropolitan high schools and a dropout rate of one in four. It was virtually certain right from the very start that the students at this school wouldn't listen to any speech on the "road ahead." For an instant, the image of me futilely addressing a bunch of twenty-year-olds at a coming-of-age ceremony flitted through my mind. Why, then, didn't I simply refuse?

Prior to this I had spoken at many different places about my thoughts on the circumstances under which young people work, along the lines that I have written in this book. In almost every case, however, the people whom I had addressed so far were adults. The youngest were first-year college students. I had never spoken to high school students.

I had no intention in this book of stirring up a generational conflict between young people and middle-aged and older workers over employment issues. Even though the root of the conflict is a system that protects surplus middle-aged and older employees, I do not believe that wantonly destroying that system would do any good. Young people find themselves in a situation in which nothing comes of trying hard; my motive, if you could call it that, in writing this book is to provide some tiny bit of information that might help dispel some of the vague uneasiness that young people feel and give them a clear view of the realities they face so that they can fight coolly at work without aimlessly and needlessly trying hard. I had never once said any of these things to high school or junior high school students, however. Perhaps I thought it wouldn't do any good because teenagers have already given up needlessly worrying themselves about such things. And yet I would never know for sure unless I tried.

The speech that I planned to give was what I have written here, explained in terms that were as easy to understand as possible. Even in simplified form, however, it was probably still too difficult for high school students to understand. What it needed, I think, was more specific examples. Did the high school students listen quietly to my speech? Of course not. In order to make myself heard over the din, I found myself yelling out, "Don't try hard!" "It's all right not to have a dream!" "Become your own boss!" After it was all over, one of the students said, "I don't know what he was talking about, but it was funny watching him yelling and getting red in the face like some drunk." That was probably an honest impression. In fact, I think that just about sums it up.

Although the speech I gave was of no consequence, one thing probably was a success. I had invited some of my seminar students to come to the high school with me, and a dozen or so actually came along. After my talk had ended, the students were divided up into six groups and a couple of college students joined each group so that the high school students and the college students had a chance to talk to one another. They may have talked about work and school, but mostly it was about more immediate concerns: whether they had girlfriends or boyfriends, whether the psychic photography on a TV program was real or not, that sort of thing. Hardly any college students had ever visited this school since almost none of its graduates had gone on to college. As a result, the only chance that these had to speak directly to college students was at their part-time jobs. It's not just a matter of high school students and college students having no opportunity to speak to one another; the students at this school have virtually no chance to talk to any full-fledged members of society other than their own parents on topics that go beyond common interests. "At our school lots of people from here go out into the world, but very few from the outside world ever come in," the teacher who gave me the chance to speak told me. The important thing was that an adult had made the effort to come here and speak.

College preparatory schools are open to society. But at other schools an enormous wall separates students and adults. No one decides just for the fun of it to go and give a talk at schools that have many problems and where the students don't listen. Nevertheless, it is up to adults to break down this wall. In the process, it would also be a good thing to eliminate the distinction in the Japanese language between members of society *(shakaijin)* and students *(gakusei* or *seito)*. Students, too, are members of society.

I suspect that the teacher who asked me to speak probably honestly didn't have any expectations about my speech to begin with. What was needed thing was that I personally go to the school. Even though he didn't think I'd get my message across, he knew I would keep on talking without giving up.

There were a few things I noticed when I joined the circles of high school and college students. One of them was that, surprisingly, the seventeen-year-olds who had actually heard what I was saying were the ones who sat in the back and talked loudly with their friends during my speech. "He said, 'Don't try hard,' 'Don't have a dream,'" one of them told a college student, "but if you don't try hard, you can't make your dream come true. That's weird. He's wrong." The ones for us to worry about may be the seventeen-year-olds who sat quietly by themselves up in front. The message "become your own boss" never got through to them. I hope they don't all become solitary freeters.

Having visited a high school for only a few hours on a single day, I am unqualified to speak about today's high school students. Yet, it is true that they left a clear impression on me. The students I met, both those who wore flashy clothes and hairstyles and those who did not, were all surprisingly open and trusting. Maybe I was prejudiced. High school students with lots of problems surely, I thought, would be somehow twisted and jaded. The teacher at the school told me, "Our kids gave up worrying right from the outset." Certainly, they may have given up worrying consciously. But, at the same time, faced with a reality they can't change, they feel the bleakness of the situation with surprising candor. They also realize there is no future in being a freeter.

I am not going to generalize about seventeen-year-olds on the basis of the fewer than 200 of them I encountered at this school. The situation in which each high school student finds him/herself is utterly unique. But what they all seem to have in common is their far too ready acceptance of the status quo. This is giving rise not to anger at the situation in which they find themselves but rather to resignation and a feeling of helplessness. That is the reason—their very trustingness is the reason—that I ended up blurting out, "Don't let yourselves be cheated."

It would be a lie, of course, to say that they would never be cheated if they became full-time employees. The number of young full-time employees who work extremely hard for longer hours than what economics would describe as rational behavior far exceeds the number of freeters. However, the probability of freeters being cheated, taken advantage of, and overworked is overwhelmingly higher than it is for full-time employees. That is the reason I want to tell them to be more cunning.

The students who heard my clumsy speech in the gymnasium that day will probably never pick up this book. Young people say they have no future in society. Certainly, it is difficult for young people to imagine a future that involves growth and development. But they do have a future in society that involves maturity. It is said that for Japanese soccer to reach the world's top level, it needs to have more *malicia*. *Malicia* is a

Portuguese and Spanish word that means "cunning." It also means "tough." If young people acquire more shrewdness, they should have a future in which they will be tougher and more mature than previous generations.

In conclusion, a high school student that day asked me a direct question: "As a college professor, how much do you make?" For some reason I hesitated and was unable to tell him the truth. "College professors probably are paid lots more than high school teachers," the student said, "but teaching high school is much harder." Let me speak frankly. My salary for August 2001 was 420,200 yen. In addition I receive numerous benefits. Compared to a high school teacher of the same age who has to contend with high school students every day, my pay may indeed be too high. But I was unable to say with pride what I really feel about my salary—that it is fair to receive that much money because I work hard for it. I regret not having said that.

Grown-ups are quick to say that they rest their hopes on young people, who are the future of society. But if they really feel that way, they will have to provide in good faith (even if only lightheartedly) the information that young people want to know. They will also have to think about what sort of information is really useful. In order to do that, each of us will have to ask ourselves whether we take any pride in our work—just a little will do! In the final analysis, the issue is not how young people will work in the future, but how adults are working right now.

The young generation and the middle-aged and older generation are snatching a limited number of jobs away from one another. The latter in particular are robbing young people of employment opportunities in order to protect their own jobs as a vested right, a situation that is steadily intensifying. The reason young people are becoming freeters and parasite singles has nothing to do with a decline in their work ethic. Rather, it is a result of the fact that they have been deprived of meaningful jobs. On the other hand, more and more young people who work as full-time employees are putting in excessively long hours in a performance-based pay system that makes no provisions for training; as a result, they are losing their incentive to work.

To resolve this situation, of course, the government and the schools need to come up with policies, but, above all, each of us must change the relationship between ourselves and our present jobs. A big factor behind the rising sense of job insecurity is the ambivalent relationship people have to their work. Even though, essentially, work that did not turn out well is not evaluated, still, job performance reviews make people feel that their value as human beings is being denied. There is something of this in Japanese society.

The first step toward improving this situation is to talk about our jobs in our own words and with a modicum of pride. A person who cannot do this won't be able to get a new job despite his/her abilities. If meaningful job opportunities are on the wane, people should begin working for themselves and determine the nature of their own jobs, in short, they should "become their own boss." To become your own boss or to succeed in changing jobs, a wide circle of relationships with people whom you can consult outside the home and workplace will be a strong weapon. A good job is impossible to find if you simply commute back and forth between home and work.

A vague, nagging sense of job insecurity. What is the best way to deal with that uneasiness and coolly fight it? The editor who recommended that I write this book asked me to write a book that "could give readers a real sense of the things that they instinctively feel about work but that, in fact, are linked to various economic and social trends." Whether this book has met that expectation, I cannot say. I leave that up to the reader to decide.

# *Acknowledgments*

As I stated at the beginning, the basis for my thinking in this book are the data. The research given in the sections entitled "The data speak" at the end of certain chapters all use data that would not have been available to me without my participation in a government-affiliated research group. I would like to express my gratitude to the other participants in this group and to the members of the secretariat for giving me the opportunity to do these analyses. In particular, I would like to thank Satō Hiroki, Takeuchi Eiji, Higuchi Yoshio, and Morishima Motohiro, who organized the study group and recommended that I join it.

On the other hand, it is also a fact that I could never have written this book as an analysis of the data alone. In that sense, the people whom I met while doing group research from 1998 to 2001 at the Personnel and Labour Course (now the Human Resource Management Course) in the business academy run by the Japan Productivity Center for Socio-Economic Development have been very important to me. These are people who give serious thought to the nature of the company, the nature of work, and their relationship to the individual, and almost every week I discussed ideas, exchanged e-mails, and went drinking with them. Without these experiences I could probably never have written this book. It was here that I truly experienced the importance of "weak ties" with friends you can count on even though you meet infrequently, a topic that I have emphasized here repeatedly. Many parts of this book, it would be fair to say, are the result of the joint research I did with them. I would like to take this opportunity to thank them all.

In addition, I would like to thank Mr. Katō and Mr. Suzuki for making the opportunity for me to speak at their high school. I am sincerely grateful to them both for allowing me to have that invaluable experience and to the seventeen-year-olds there who taught me so many different things.

I have worked at Gakushūin University for ten years beginning in 1992. The seminar students whom I met there and the members of the Faculty of Economics' joint research center who supported my lectures and my research were the young people in their twenties who have been closest to me. My thanks in particular to Takahashi Yōko and Kawakami Atsushi of Gakushūin, who carefully read over my manuscript, made frank comments about its contents and mode of expression, and compiled the index. If this book has become somewhat more reader friendly, it is thanks to the two of them.

The basis for this book are the ideas I have been thinking about since 1998 in a number of articles I have written for various journals. I would like to thank all the members of their editorial staffs and publications departments for responding positively to my requests. Finally, I want to say thank you once again to Yoshida Daisaku of Chuokoron-Shinsha who was in charge of editing this book and who contributed many ideas to its organization and presentation.

Genda Yūji
November 2001

# Index

**G**



**H**



**I**



**J**



**K**



**L**



**M**

**O**

CANCELLED
JUN 0 1 2006